A School in Kenya:

Hospital Hill

1949–1973

A School in Kenya:
Hospital Hill
1949–1973

Joan Karmali

A Square One Publication

First published in 2002 by
Square One Publications
The Tudor House
16 Church Street
Upton on Severn
Worcestershire
WR8 0HT

© 2002 Joan Karmali

British Library Cataloguing in Publication Data is available for this book

ISBN 1 877755 49 6

Typeset by Avon DataSet Ltd, Bidford on Avon B50 4JH
Printed in Great Britain by Biddles Ltd, Guildford

Acknowledgemetns

When Hospital Hill School was taken over by Nairobi City Council at the beginning of 1973 the teachers were determined that its records should not be lost. Several of them – and sadly I cannot now recall all their names – brought all the old school files to our house for safekeeping. John and I already had files of our own, of early correspondence and minutes of governors' meetings as well as many photographs. I have thus had access to a wealth of information as well as my own memories, and I should like to record my deep appreciation of the loyalty of all Hospital Hill's staff over the years. Had it not been for the devotion of those who rescued the files, much less would be known about the school. In 1986 John and I moved to a smaller house and then for want of room had to jettison the school registers, but everything else, including many press cuttings, has been preserved.

While writing the book I was able to contact the few ex-HHS pupils whose addresses I knew and almost without exception they wrote to me with memories of their days at the school from which I have quoted. I am deeply indebted to them. I wish there had been more.

John and I are very grateful to Hal and Marjorie Partridge for sharing with us their memories of Mrs Eileen Walke, of her problems in the Kenya of the day and of her continuing devotion to the ideal of a non-racist society – and also for the warm hospitality they extended to us in their home in Malta.

As many of the photographs in the book were taken nearly fifty years ago it is impossible to acknowledge accurately who the individual photographers were. However, I can say that among them were Nand Kishore Sapra; Fantasia Photographers; Duncan Whitfield; Freddie Yowell; and photographers from East African Newspapers Ltd. The wonderful set from the early days of Hospital Hill School in Government House grounds when Mrs Walke was headmistress were taken at the instigation of John Reiss, (father of the first European pupils at that site), who was at the time the British Colonial Office's Information Officer for East Africa. Some of the more personal ones were of course taken by individuals, including John and me.

I have acknowledged in the text the source of Stanley Meisler's reportage of the school's PTA meeting in 1973 and hope the Los Angeles Times will forgive me (in my eighties), for not being able to seek their permission to quote.

Mary Wilkinson of Square One Publications has been most encouraging and supportive with practical suggestions and I thank her warmly for this.

Finally I should like to thank my husband John; my children, Jan, Peter and Shereen; and Loretta Tremlett for their helpful suggestions and recollections, and to Shereen in particular for her invaluable assistance, both editorial and practical, in finalising the manuscript, without which I doubt I should have completed it.

Foreword

An explanation is necessary as to why what purports to be an account of a school which originated in Africa in 1949, actually starts during the Second World War in Britain. This was when my husband and I met and when our resolve to fight against any racial prejudice we met with was crystallised. This resolution was one of the factors which led to the existence of Hospital Hill School.

To understand why the school seemed so distinctive at the time, its story must be set in the environment of the day. I have attempted to do this by setting it within my own personal memoir. As will become apparent, many other people, to a greater or lesser degree, made very significant, often indispensable, contributions to establishing and maintaining Hospital Hill, especially to the spirit and ethos which distinguished it.

To John, for sixty happy years

Introduction

As we all struggle with the challenges of the 21st century it is easy to forget how rapidly the world has changed. I am one of those who can spend hours reading about the past and it is always a delight to find books that touch on events and places where I have a personal memory. This book by Joan Karmali is one such account and I am sure that many, particularly those with a Kenya connection, will find it both interesting and charming.

Kenya's experiences during the first half of the 20th Century were typical of a British colony. Segregation and policies of government were founded on race although the system of 'apartheid' never became established, there was certainly sympathy for the concept on the part of the colonial authorities. Today, Kenya remains remarkably free of racial tensions and this is to a very large extent the result of efforts by people such as John and Joan Karmali.

It is tempting to give all the credit to a particular development and obviously Kenya's success in overcoming racial barriers is a complex story. Nonetheless, I do believe that the primary school started and developed by the Karmalis played a most fundamental role in shaping the Kenya of today. Nairobi's Hospital Hill School was a special place and a large number of Kenya's business and community leaders benefited enormously from this 'mixed race' education. The details of this schools origin and growth is fascinating and represents an important part of our nation's past. Although I did not go to the Hospital Hill Primary School, I have known many people from widely different backgrounds who did. The impact upon their early moulding is obvious and underscores the enormous importance of 'starting early' to establish personal values and standards. I know this remains a matter of debate amongst educators but I believe that the preteen years are amongst the most important in forming social attitudes. Racism and prejudice is learned both at home and at school.

In addition to the school, John and Joan had wide interests and they made many important contributions. I am delighted that Joan has written this book and it is a great pleasure to have contributed this brief introduction.

Richard Leakey

Prologue

Life in North Wales

When my father was called up in the First World War he was graded C3, not only having defective eyesight but also a heart murmur. Consequently he was never posted overseas. A bright young man, he had been forced to leave school early, aged just 14, because for some unaccountable reason his father, previously a pious Baptist, had taken to drink and there was no longer any money for school fees. Recently, a television programme on life in Britain in the 1900s revealed that many amateur photographers of the time died or became mysteriously ill or mad due to absorption of cyanide from the chemicals used to develop or fix their films. My grandfather was a seriously keen amateur photographer, doing all his own processing, and I am convinced that must have been the cause of his defection. I like to think the stain can now be removed from the family tree! He had died in Gloucester Infirmary allegedly from delirium tremens.

My father was apprenticed to the tailoring trade and it was in this capacity that he served in the army. When he was posted to Kinmel Camp in North Wales he had been married for several years and so that he and my mother could be together in his free time, they took rooms in Rhyl. Here, within sound of the sea and a few weeks after the armistice, I was born, and in this seaside resort I spent the first 20 years of my life. Rhyl was distinguished mainly for its long promenade and sandy beaches and an influx of day trippers during the summer season.

When demobilised, my father had set up a business as a 'bespoke' tailor and outfitter and for some years did well. But his business slowly suffered by competition from bigger firms selling cheaper products, such as Montague Burton, and was hit even harder by the recession of the 1930s. Several years earlier the dancing lessons I loved and piano lessons I didn't, had ceased, but it was my mother who suffered most, darning and scrimping, always striving to maintain an aura of genteel respectability, the hallmark of the times. Bread and butter became bread and margarine, then bread and scrape. I have a particularly vivid memory of being sent to buy a quarter of margarine with a silver shilling which had a hole in it, taken from a charm bracelet of my mother's. The man in the Maypole, a kindly soul, clearly regretted having to refuse this gawky embarrassed child. The bracelet itself soon disappeared, along with other ornaments of my mother's, gold brooches and bracelets, and my father's gold hunter watch, sold to itinerant opportunists who, I felt even then, undoubtedly paid below their true value. My parents were staunch Conservatives and during the good times had been members of the local club. When fortune ceased to smile upon them so, it seemed, did their fellow Conservatives, something my mother felt deeply.

School days

Fortunately Christ Church elementary school was only four minutes walk (two minutes run, my usual mode of progression) from our home in Sussex Street. Under the deceptively gentle headship of Mrs E.E. Hughes, whose charm was underwritten by organisational skills and an iron will, it had the reputation of being the best in town. It did me proud and, aged 11, I managed to come top of the district in the entrance exams for the next stage of education, so gaining the scholarship without which I should have gone no further. Rhyl County School had just appointed a new headmaster, T. I. Ellis, Oxford graduate and posthumous son of much loved Welsh nationalist leader Tom Ellis. T.I. devoted his considerable energies to extra-curricular activities for the boys but the girls, with one exception, were totally neglected in this respect.

School provided some escape from the rather stifling atmosphere at home but I was to tap an even richer vein of happiness when a school-friend, Margaret Roberts, enthused one day about the activities at her Congregational chapel, also called Christ Church. Its dynamic pastor, the Reverend Ambrose Evans, inspired his congregation with a sense of service so that in addition to an excellent choir and a Sunday school, they variously ran a Guide company (the 5th Rhyl), an amateur dramatic company, which put on shows of considerable merit in the Pavilion each year, and in summer a thriving tennis club.

Eventually my parents, one a devout Anglican and the other a lapsed Baptist, agreed to allow me to attend its Sunday school so that I could join their Girl Guide company. There was a warmth of community there which I had never experienced before and found particularly enriching. There I managed to acquire a few social skills and, from the nature-loving Guide captain (the virtually anonymous Miss Jones), an ability to identify the commoner birds, trees and wildflowers which were then to be seen in abundance on our Saturday treks.

In one of their Christmas pantomimes I was a rather skinny-looking Fairy Queen, but my most memorable moment was receiving praise in the local paper when, aged about 14, I played the part of Mary in the Easter passion play. Looking back, I see I must have been profoundly influenced subliminally by a picture hanging in the church hall, where Guide meetings and other activities took place, of a group of children of all nationalities and colours gathered round a seated Christ, implying as it did that we are all of equal value in the sight of God.

Financially things at home went from bad to worse and to keep us going my mother resorted to taking in boarders. In the summer these were families from Lancashire or the Midlands who stayed for a week or two, but in time we moved to a larger pleasanter house in Bath Street, and several unmarried teachers from the secondary school lodged with us in term time. Naturally I helped with the additional housework. Simultaneous resentment at this intrusion into our home-life, and guilt at harbouring such feelings while my mother was striving to keep the family going, added to the usual stresses of adolescence.

The frustrated chemist

My father loved to relate how as a small boy, the youngest of the family by 10 years, he had enjoyed helping his father in his twin hobbies of photography (glass plates and buckets of chemicals!) and a study of herbs. The second had rubbed off on my father and he treasured a well-worn copy of Culpepper's Herbal. When I was small I can recall the house being filled from time to time with the odours of quillaia or cinchona bark, boiling away in the kitchen to produce some obscure concoctions, to my mother's evident annoyance. He was a frustrated chemist and was determined that I should take the path which had been denied to him. I was besotted by the poetry of Wordsworth, Keats and Browning and longed to go to university to study English or history, but as we were penniless, that was a forlorn hope. If taking science subjects would lead to an assured and reasonably well-paid career, I was prepared to go that way. But pharmacy, a worthy and essential profession, hardly broadens the mind or nourishes the spirit. Nonetheless I am eternally grateful to my farsighted father for instilling in me the resolve to get an education somehow, some way. In his generation it was unusual to encourage girls to do this and, as a result perhaps, while I believe deeply that women should have equal opportunities and access to education and top-ranking jobs, I have never dwelt on the wilder shores of feminism.

After four years as a scholarship girl (*a la* Richard Hoggart) at Rhyl County School I was apprenticed for three years to a local chemist. It was not a satisfactory apprenticeship. I learnt little, and from the five, 10, and 15 shillings a week I earned in successive years it was impossible to make significant savings. Most winter evenings after the shop closed, I trudged to night-classes in chemistry, physics and botany, usually too tired to take much in. My self-esteem took a beating.

Then things looked up. With the apprenticeship behind me, I discovered that I could take a year's course for the entrance exam to college at Colwyn Bay secondary school, a mere 12 miles away so that I could travel daily by train. I was 19, and this proved to be a wonderful year. In every respect Colwyn Bay was several notches ahead of Rhyl County and its science master, T.O.Griffiths (inevitably known as Toggy to his students), was a brilliant teacher. He made physics intelligible, but his greatest gift was to believe in me, to boost my self confidence. Go for the top, he said. You can make it. Under his guidance I applied to London university instead of the rather seedy college in Liverpool to which all other local pharmacy students aspired.

Still with no idea how I should get to university to qualify as a pharmacist, I was again fortunate, this time in having a wonderfully caring school friend, Gwyneth Haynes-Thomas. Probably rather cleverer than I, she had failed to gain entry to Lady Margaret Hall but had won a place at the University of Manchester. Knowing how depressed I was about my future prospects, she arranged an interview for me (how, I do not know!) with her university's advisor to women students. This most helpful woman put me in touch with the Pioneer and Soroptimists women's societies – and suddenly, everything had become possible. On the basis of one interview these splendid women had, in 1939, allocated me interest-free loans of £100 and £120 respectively, which paid my fees and maintenance for a year at university.

War-time England

It was one of those summers we all seem to remember from childhood, the kind of days which normally lift the spirits. The sun was brilliant, the sky cloudless, but in no way did the news match the weather. Even we raised our heads from our books and copious notes for long enough to register that German tanks were sweeping through France.

It was May 1940, the time of Dunkirk and the epic evacuation by any craft which was seaworthy of the retreating British Army from the continent of Europe. Churchill replaced Chamberlain as Prime Minister and warned the nation that invasion could be imminent. What did the future hold for any of us? We could not guess, but imagined various horrors. For now, we could only concentrate on work and passing our exams.

John Karmali and I, Joan Organ, were two of some 120 students of the College of the Royal Pharmaceutical Society, a part of the University of London which, at the outbreak of war, had been evacuated to Cardiff. John was in his last year, I in my first. In such a small college we all got to know each other well and spent what leisure we had on communal activities, going on rambles in the not-so-distant countryside, to the occasional concert, and dances at the Students Union. Often after long evenings over our books, we would run a circuit round Cardiff's beautiful city centre to loosen up our muscles and clear our heads, sharing banter and a bag of chips (fish was definitely 'off') on the way back to our various digs. By the time the phoney war was over John and I, with so many shared interests, had developed a close friendship, fallen in love, and were considering marriage.

In 1935 on an icy morning in December, John, aged 17, born and raised in Kenya, had arrived at Victoria station in London, having travelled by cattle-boat to Marseilles, then, through the kindly guidance of a fellow traveller, by train across France and on to London. Here he was met by a representative of his family's business agents, and deposited at the Indian Students Union in Gower Street. With only the assurance of a small monthly allowance, he was now on his own, committed to finding himself a suitable college to pursue a career in pharmacy, and somewhere more satisfactory to live, both of which, in a totally unfamiliar environment, he achieved with considerable skill, all within budget.

For us, marriage would not be easy. John was Indian, I English. Both our families, in the thinking of that pre-war time warp, would be against our marriage, as would many others. But we had a profound conviction that the flow of history would prove to be with us. John I knew to be a man of fearless integrity, one of the most honourable and upright people I had ever met, besides being intelligent and at times very funny. His irreverent sense of humour, especially in those dark days of war, I found very appealing. My sense of justice was offended by the suggestion that because he had a brown skin, he was 'inferior'. It was merely that he had more melanin in his skin than I had in mine.

So for now, we thought, let's just qualify. Whatever the war's outcome, if we are still alive and free, we shall at least be equipped to earn a living. If Germany invaded successfully, John, so obviously non-Aryan, would face imprisonment, torture and death. We must grasp life and live it fully while we could.

That summer, exams behind us, John began his year's apprenticeship at a chemists in Notting Hill Gate and I, now a chemist and druggist, a member of the Pharmaceutical Society, spent the summer working as a locum in Wrexham. The pharmacy was called Rowlands and Co, but was owned by Knox Mawer who was a member of Council of the Pharmaceutical Society. He had turned down my application for a grant while I was still an apprentice in Rhyl, but as the best student of the year, I had won the Greenish Scholarship and the Martindale Medal, and he snapped me up. Now I had the funds enabling me to return to Cardiff in the autumn and study for the higher qualification of pharmaceutical chemist, which later elevated me to the status of fellow of the Royal Pharmaceutical Society.

Going for the higher qualification was also by courtesy of the Pioneer Society and the Soroptimists of Greater London, to each of which organisations I owed money. Repayment of these loans should have begun that summer but both societies agreed to postpone payment for another year. They hardly knew me and I am eternally grateful to them for the opportunity they gave me, for my parents were in no position to help me financially.

Several times in the winter of 1940/41 I went up to see John in London. There and in Cardiff we each had narrow escapes from bombs falling nearby. In August 1941 I began work in Kings Langley in the Ovaltine Research Laboratories, on finding alternative sources of essential vitamins and methods of standardising them. Proposed by my boss, Dr Frank Wokes, I was elected to the Biochemical and Nutrition Societies. In the next few years we published a number of papers in various scientific journals, including *Nature*, collaborating on several projects with scientists working at the Dunn Nutrition Laboratories in Cambridge. Frankie Wokes was a kindly, mildly eccentric character, a vegetarian who habitually dressed in knee breeches and long socks. He never used joined-up writing, but wrote out all his papers by hand in small print, for subsequent typing. His ambition was to equal his counterpart at Glaxo Research Laboratories, a brilliant polymath, A. L. Bacharach, whose research into nutrition involved using experimental animals. This was totally opposed to Wokes's principles and we used only chemical and physical chemical methods to assess the vitamin contents of foods.

Marriage

Towards the end of 1943 John and I married. My father, still hoping to dissuade me from marriage, had stubbornly refused to come to my wedding so we had decided to keep the occasion small. On a Friday we went to a Muslim mosque in Ealing for the ceremony which would satisfy John's parents, (at that time there was no Ismaili mosque in Britain), and on the next day had the civil ceremony at Ealing registry office. My mother, sister, and John's cousin Shamsu Ahamed, who at that time was a student at LSE, were our witnesses. Our flat was the upper part of a house owned by Mr and Mrs Newbutt who had become wonderfully supportive friends and Mrs Newbutt made and iced our wedding cake, using the *sine qua non*, precious dried fruit sent from Kenya by John's family.

Eventually even my father became reconciled to my marriage, though remaining apprehensive about my life in Kenya. John had a moral obligation to return and set up a chemist's business in Nairobi as planned, which his three younger brothers were expected to join after suitable training.

For much of the war, correspondence between the UK and Kenya had been impossible. When things improved John wrote a long letter to his parents, the timing of which proved to be particularly felicitous. His family were of the Ismaili faith, the Shia Muslim sect led by the Aga Khan. The then Imam was a sophisticated, far-seeing religious leader, of ample stature and corresponding wealth, best known in the wider world for his success in breeding racehorses, three of which in the 1930s won the Derby. This, combined with his generosity and great personal charm, the British public found very endearing. During John's stay in England, he had, when there, acted as his guardian.

When the all-important letter arrived in Nairobi, the Aga's elder son, Prince Aly Khan, who had spent much of the war with the British forces based in East Africa, happened to be on safari with John's father. Prince Aly's wife and two young sons, the elder of whom, Prince Karim, was destined eventually to succeed his grandfather, lived in Nairobi during most of the war, and when Aly had a few days leave in the capital, John's father acted as his 'secretary', poker-playing companion, and driver.

On being shown John's letter, Prince Aly immediately sent us a cable of congratulations, and made clear to the family that he and his father were entirely in favour of Ismailis, if they so wished, marrying out of the community. How this smoothed our path!

As a child I had longed to travel and see the world so I looked forward with excitement to living in Kenya. Clearly, it would not be a bed of roses. Before I agreed to marry him John had explained to me very fully that segregation as severe as that in South Africa existed in Kenya. The will and interests of white settlers were considered paramount by colonial government servants. Theoretically, it must be said, this was not British government policy, but settler influence was strong, and they were on the spot.

Education in the colony, where it existed, had been racially segregated from the very start. As early as 1904 the railways ran two schools in Nairobi for their staff. They were next door to each other, but one was for Europeans and one for Africans, albeit with a single headmaster, A.J. Turner. Government took these over in 1910 but until 1911 there was much opposition by the Europeans to educating Africans, and only missionaries had provided schools for African children. From that date, government did allocate grants to some mission schools, and by 1926 it was deemed that they had produced sufficient pupils to justify providing secondary education for these few. The setting up of the Alliance High School in Kikuyu was one outcome of this decision. It is notable that in

Uganda, where the only Europeans were colonial servants, either civil or medical, and where settler influence was virtually absent, education for Africans had been introduced 20 years earlier. Settlers attitudes seemed to me to indicate so fragile a sense of their own worth that they clung for dear life to the notion that a white skin conferred superiority.

John and I would not be able to go together into hotels or restaurants. Only during the war had segregation on the trains and in cinemas been relaxed a little. No European, I was told, would wish to know me. It would be considered that I had 'let the side down' and I must sink or swim without any support from the European community, who quite clearly believed that, disillusioned and unhappy, I should soon disappear without trace. My reaction to this was one of contempt for those whites who refused to mix with Africans and Asians on grounds of colour. On those of education and interests I understood that a lack of common ground would discourage mixing. But because of colour? Never. Where he would be refused entrance, there I too was happy not to go.

To Kenya

In February 1946 John and I set off for Kenya with our first son, Jan, who had been born in May 1945, eight days after VE Day. We went with mixed emotions, sadness on my part to be leaving family and friends, happiness for John at the prospect of reunion with his – and mutual pleasure at putting behind us the horrors of war, memories of nights spent in air-raid shelters hearing the whine and 'crump' of bombs falling all around us. Many people we had known were killed or maimed. Ever after, in moments when problems seemed overwhelming, we reminded ourselves how fortunate we were just to be alive. The *S.S.Franconia* was still half a troop ship but the rest of her accommodation was allocated to civilians like John, returning to their homes and families after the long separation of the war years.

Once through the Bay of Biscay life on the ship was pure bliss. Better fed than for years – we each weighed little more than 100 pounds – we cruised through the Mediterranean in brilliant sunshine. At last I understood why my favourite colour was called aquamarine. The grey sea of my home town, Rhyl, had borne no resemblance to the brilliant blue shadings of this one. The baby gurgled happily in his pram, adored by some young soldiers clearly missing their own families. And to my delight, flying fishes flew.

Accommodation on board the *Franconia* was limited and crowded. Male civilians, some 50 or so of them, slept in hammocks in large communal cabins, wives and children in another. Only two small two-berth cabins were available, and one of these, with considerable sensitivity, was allocated to John, baby Jan, and me. It felt like the beginning of a great adventure. And it was.

After three weeks we awoke early one morning to the realisation that the ship was stationary. Rushing on deck we were met by the sight of white sands fringed with palm trees fingered by gentle breezes, the idyllic Kenya coast, totally unspoilt, not a soul in sight. The cognoscenti informed us that we could proceed no further without a pilot. Soon, with him on board, the ship slowly traversed the narrow Mida Creek, to dock at Mombasa's deep-water Kilindini Harbour.

Passengers lined the rails, eagerly looking for familiar faces among the people waiting on the dock. 'Oh', shrieked a teenage passenger, in what my mother would have described as a 'common' voice, 'look at those gypsies!' She was pointing at two girls in brilliant saris, standing with a tall, strikingly handsome man – two of John's sisters and his father, Bapa, commonly known outside his family as 'K'.

Down the gangway we went, into their arms. The girls wept with joy and disbelief at being reunited with their brother after 11 years. Ten month-old Jan was snatched into their arms and smothered with kisses, which he initially viewed with some dismay. My father-in-law greeted me warmly, and quickly he and the girls whisked us away by car, leaving his two sons-in-law to the task of clearing our baggage through customs.

The next few days are somewhat hazy in my memory. My sister-in-law Sherin and her husband lived with his widowed mother in Mombasa, and this is where we stayed. I was over-whelmed by the warmth with which we were welcomed by everyone we met, and Bapa clearly delighted in showing us off to his coastal friends. No Europeans of course, but lovely Ismaili families and some Ithnashris, another small Muslim sect, all successful businessmen at the coast. For several hundred years trading had gone on between the east coast of Africa and the west coast of India, and of course with Arabia. Permanent immigrants had not settled till towards the end of the 19th century though there had been some infiltration by intermarriage. Until the advent of modern medicine, populations had remained small.

K wanted to prolong his coast holiday, but we were anxious to get on, up to Nairobi, John to see his mother who during his absence had totally lost her sight; and I because there had been cases of measles on board ship and I wanted to reach base and reliable medical facilities in case Jan should fall sick.

The overnight train left Mombasa about six, and we three had a four-berth coupe next door to K's. The contrast to life in Britain was unimaginable. Genial Africans came to transform our comfortable benches into beds, with blankets, pillows and stiffly starched sheets. With Jan fed and settled we moved next door where K was already entertaining friends, and the whiskey flowed freely. The train rumbled on into the night, straining up the incline, though we had had a farewell glimpse before darkness fell of the palm-lined beaches. An African ayah (nanny), sat with sleeping Jan while we walked along to the dining car and ate a splendid meal off tables brilliant with white napery, crystal glass and heavy silver, yet another contrast with wartime Britain. Perhaps I ate too quickly to fully appreciate the delights of fresh prawns, fish and tender young vegetables, but I was anxious to get back to Jan, not quite trusting, with fears which proved groundless, his unfamiliar ayah.

Dawn came early. We'd slept surprisingly well in spite of various halts and mysterious shuntings during the night, and it was special to be wakened with a tray of tea and biscuits delivered to our coupe. Washed and dressed, we consumed an excellent breakfast, which Jan seemed to enjoy while watching in wide-eyed wonder the strange people, movement and colour all around him.

We pulled into Nairobi station about 8 a.m. In mid-platform was a large group of young men and women, gathered around a short, plump older woman, patcheri (shawl) over her head, who seemed to be gazing anxiously along the length of the train. But those eyes were blind. She was dependent on the commentary of her youngest son, who held her arm.

15

The train stopped, and we tumbled out. Although, or perhaps because, there had been minimum communication for 11 years, this reunion was charged with emotion. These were no stiff-upper-lipped Brits, but people accustomed to expressing their emotions uninhibitedly. There were tears, laughter, hugs and kisses. Jan wailed and had to be restored to my arms. Most poignant of all was the sight of John's mother, tears streaming down her cheeks, moving her hands delicately over his face, trying to identify the features of her eldest child, unseen for 11 years, never to be seen again. And all the time uttering little cries of thanks to her God for returning this beloved child to her.

Fortunately I was able to identify almost all these members of my new family from the photos they had sent to John over the last few months. And I was deeply touched by their loving welcome to this stranger in their midst.

Family life in Parklands

We piled into several cars and drove to the family home in Parklands. Racial segregation in Kenya applied to where one could and could not live. Many areas of Nairobi – the pleasantest ones of course – were 'restricted', meaning that only Europeans could purchase property or live in them. Initial settlements at the turn of the century had transformed the small area at the railhead, known to the Maasai as Nairobi, 'place of pleasant waters', into a township. It was mainly a shanty town but gradually some sort of roads appeared, notably Government Road. There was a bazaar area with small shops and stalls owned by Indians, and soon what became Nairobi's celebrated hotels, the Norfolk and the Stanley, later the New Stanley.

Those white settlers who could, moved out a mile or so to build their homes. Parklands and Westlands were two of the first suburbs. In the 1920s and1930s as Asian businessmen grew wealthier, they too moved out from slum areas like River Road, where John was born, and infiltrated Parklands. The Europeans moved further afield, to Riverside Drive – a world away from River Road! – and Muthaiga, and it was no doubt then that restrictive clauses were introduced into property deeds by the Europeans who ran things, to forestall further infiltration.

Karmali Mohamed, John's father, known to his friends as 'K', had bought a 5-acre plot in Parklands which extended across from Second to Third Avenues and had two houses on it. A magnificent avenue of mature jacaranda trees ran through the garden from road to road so that in November when they flowered one could hardly bear to walk on and crush the carpet of pale mauve blossoms. John's parents, three young brothers and youngest unmarried sister, occupied the big house, with his ancient widowed grandmother, Dadima, in an annexe. Fifty yards or so away the smaller house had been furnished for us with imported bedroom suite, sofa, chairs, table, and a cot for Jan. (Locally made furniture was considered inferior and probably was at that time. 'Imported' conferred a certain cachet). The girls had been to considerable trouble to find pretty blue curtains and chintz covers, making it as homelike as possible. There was a bathroom – but only outside sanitation, common to most houses in the country at that time. The side of the garden which bounded the road had a tall kei-apple hedge, intended to deter thieves, but since the wide open gateway lacked a gate, its fearsomely long pointed thorns served as a hazard only to those, who eventually included our children, unwary enough to run around without shoes.

Most of the luggage we had brought from England consisted of hundreds of books, and K soon arranged for his favourite *fundi* (Swahili for handyman) to come in and make bookcases to fit round the walls of the little room we planned to convert into a study. We were secretly amused (though also grateful) that he had overcome his early antipathy to books, when John as a schoolboy had had to conceal his Edgar Wallace thrillers and the like behind cushions, or have his ears boxed. For possible future reference we also had all our university notebooks which because of their size were laid flat on the tops of the bookcases.

Months later, wishing to check some obscure point, I climbed the step-ladder, to find all our thick volumes riddled with large irregular holes, making our notes indecipherable. It was our first experience of the voracity of white ants. Liberal sprinklings of pyrethrum dust and regular checking prevented any further disasters but we found this one pretty shattering. Another unwelcome discovery was that in our absence at work, K was in the habit of taking friends over to our house to show them how well accommodated we were. In itself of course, this was a loveable trait – until we began to miss some favourite books. With typical generosity he had pressed on his friends any volume they happened to admire. It was another example of the clash of cultures – as head of the family, what was ours was his. And he had paid for the bookcases. But he had no conception of how loved – and irreplaceable – favourite books could be. How could he have?

My kitchen housed a formidable Dover stove which burned wood, but my mother-in-law, known to us all as Ma, with characteristic kindness eventually donated her electric cooker to make my life easier.

The joys of Ismaili cooking

She was a magnificent cook. Soon after I met him John had told me with evident pride that she could cook for a month without once repeating a recipe. I may have been a highly qualified chemist but the few culinary skills I'd acquired as a child had hardly been enhanced by the opportunities food rationing had provided in Britain, so I was keen to learn.

I did try my hand at baking, but the oven of the Dover stove defeated my every attempt. It was a law unto itself, producing either burnt, or soggy, sunken offerings, my only success, appropriately, being the Welsh cakes I cooked on the griddle. While awaiting our arrival in Mombasa, K had taken on Juma, a Swahili man of great charm who always wore a red fez and long white khanzu, and who had agreed to come to Nairobi as our house servant. When John was out I was glad of Juma's cheerfully smiling presence but he too failed to come to terms with the Dover stove. The only thing it could do efficiently was boil, useful for making tea but not much else. The heavy charcoal iron however (another new experience for me), Juma wielded with aplomb. I soon learnt that Ma's delicious meals were produced on a 'sigri', or a series of them, small iron stoves containing red-hot charcoal, occasionally supplemented by a Primus stove.

Looking back, I seem to have spent many hours in those first weeks wandering round the house with a baby under my arm and a copy of 'Up-Country Swahili' in the other hand, endeavouring to communicate with Juma. All to no avail as within weeks Ramadan dawned, during which month complete fasting is enjoined on the faithful between dawn and dusk. Juma, a devout Muslim, neither ate nor drank even water during the day, becoming too listless to undertake any work and, what was worse, at sundown not only ate but drank the local alcoholic brew to excess. He had to go, and we took on a servant of one of the local tribes. He was pretty lugubrious and I missed Juma's beaming smile.

K had explained to us that while we would live in our own house, all meals other than breakfast would be taken in the main house, and in those early days where all was unfamiliar I was happy with this arrangement. In Indian households of the time the womenfolk cooked, and served food to the men at table, only taking their own meal when the men had finished. I became an honorary male, and was truly amazed at the wealth of delicious food brought to the table. We began with samosas, kebabs and

19

bagias. Already the table held small dishes of lime and mango pickle and kichumba, a mixture of diced tomatoes, onions, coriander leaves and green chillies in lemon juice. In deference to my uninitiated palate, chillies had been eliminated from one of them. Then a dish of spiced minced lamb topped with what looked like fried eggs, and just as I leant back, more than satisfied, in came mounds of rice, with chicken curry.

On other days we had delectable marsala fish with rotla, a dark earthy sort of chapati made from millet flour, which at first turned me off (it looked and I fancied tasted as if made of mud) but which I came to love. Then there was chicken biriani and meltingly delicious payas, sheep's trotters in a rich, hot and spicy sauce. Throughout the meal steady supplies of hot chapatis or puris came to the table, and it was to make this possible that the women remained in the kitchen, since trying to chew a cold chapati is like wrestling with a piece of rubber.

Evening meals were simpler, often leftovers from lunch, or more often kicheri, a mixture of rice and moong dahl beaten to a porridgey consistency, with a vegetable curry or khadi, which is essentially curried yoghurt. And most delicious.

Dadima and other relatives

Dadima, John's widowed grandmother, lived in a set of rooms across the terrace opposite Ma's kitchen. Traditionally she should have lived with her elder, and as it happened, considerably richer son. But his wife was a tougher customer than my gentle mother-in-law, and Dadima insisted on living in her household, a permanent thorn in the flesh. Tales abounded of the aggravation she caused poor Ma.

It was therefore amusing for me to read a quotation (headed 'Black Sheep') from Errol Trzebinski's record of Kenya's early white settlers, 'The Kenya Pioneers'. This was in Cynthia Salvadori's splendid book *We Came in Dhows*. This three volume work, in a limited edition of 2000, is a wonderful account of the Indian community's contribution to the cultural and economic development of Kenya from the end of the 19th century until the present day. Salvadori sees it as redressing the balance, since the European's contribution had already been comprehensively recorded by Elspeth Huxley and Arnold Curtis. In her book, Trzebinski speaks of Ahamed Mohamed being thrown out of India at the age of ten by his father for stealing from his mother's purse. He was sent to Kenya where his father had one contact and in time flourished greatly, being commended for his honesty at one time by the military.

My amusement was caused by the realisation that his mother was none other than the formidable Dadima of whom I was to become so fond. No wonder she refused to live in Ahamed's household. However, when her days on earth were fast running out, looking after her became too much for my blind mother-in-law, so Dadima was ultimately moved to the Ahamed's house.

Nowadays we sometimes gaze speculatively at our grand-children, hoping to detect evidence in at least one of them of entrepreneurial skills passed on through Dadima's genes! For that is surely what she was, a frustrated entrepreneur. Her wealthy elder son, Ahamed, gave her pocket-money which she considered inadequate, and undoubtedly he could well have afforded more. Determined to supplement supplies, one of her favourite tricks was to raid Ma's clothesline when the staff were otherwise occupied, and, secreting sheets or pillowcases beneath her garments, off she would go, sometimes through the hedge, and flog them to neighbouring house-servants or, may they be for-given, to the neighbours themselves. Another money-maker was to visit the grocer in Ngara where both Ahamed and Karmali families dealt, and help herself brazenly to handfuls of sweets from the screw-topped glass jars on display. Off she would go,

21

threatening the poor proprietor with sanctions should he report her to her sons, to extort a few cents from her grandchildren each time they asked for a couple of sweets. It was all profit. She was certainly a character, admirable or not!

Though we had not a syllable in common, Dadima and I developed a warm if dumb relationship, and Jan and I often sat on the lawn with her in the sun, beaming with mutual goodwill. Each day while Jan took his morning nap under the eye of his ayah, I walked over to Ma's and attempted to learn to cook by watching her at it. But she operated instinctively and I could not pin her down to exact quantities so that it was years before I really learnt, from one of her daughters. However, my Swahili quickly thrived under Ma's tuition as it was our only means of communication, and though it is a complex and beautiful language, one could navigate fairly easily through the mundane experiences of every-day without the finer points of grammar. This version, known as 'up-country' or 'kitchen' Swahili was the lingua franca of all settlers of whatever complexion. Only at the coast at that time was true, or *safi* Swahili spoken.

My sisters-in-law called me babi, the term for 'eldest brother's wife' but they already had a babi, Parin, who was the wife of their eldest cousin Jimmy Ahamed. (The concepts of 'brother' and 'first cousin' were apparently interchangeable in some circum-stances). In the early 1940s while John was in London Ahamed had sent Jimmy to Bombay in search of a wife from the pros-perous, more advanced Ismaili community there. He had done well, for Parin had a brother-in-law who was a knight.

After a day or two in Nairobi, the girls insisted on taking me to visit Parin in her impressive double-storey house on the hill. She was nearer my age and surely, I thought, we shall have much in common though I should never aspire to her legendary skills as a cook. It was a false hope, pleasant and friendly though she certainly was. To entertain her guest she asked if I should like to see her saris. Of course, I said, whereupon she opened her wardrobe to reveal row upon row of them, all the colours imaginable, in silks and chiffon, with and without borders, exactly 100 of them, more, she assured me, than any other Ismaili woman in Kenya possessed. She went on to open her safe to display a set of glittering diamonds, necklaces, bracelets, ear-rings, all the gifts of the Ahamed family on her marriage. I had, I felt, been put in my place. But though we had no common interests, Parin and I remained friendly and she could not have been kinder in sharing some of her cooking skills with me. Some of Bombay's sophistication had rubbed off on Jimmy and much of his leisure was devoted to card-playing and frequenting Nairobi's beautiful racecourse.

It would be unfair not to record that the Karmalis had indeed given me some lovely pieces of jewellery and, more valuable to me than diamonds, shares in the chemists business we eventually set up.

Long before this, in England, John and I had discussed what our life together in Kenya would be like. For me there would be two main problems. I should lack friends – and feel this lack strongly. It was not just that Europeans would reject me socially. I should never stoop to seek friendship with those I considered so unprincipled. Don't worry, said the ever-optimistic John. I have five lovely sisters, all educated, and they will make wonderful friends for you. Absence undoubtedly does make the heart grow fonder and the three youngest girls were indeed educated up to School Certificate standard, and had then trained as secretaries.

They were high-spirited, fun-loving girls, for the most part warm-hearted. In fact, had I been able to stand on the sidelines and remain uninvolved, I should have been fascinated by the whole family. They laughed, squabbled and shrieked, hugged and made up. Two of them, and the youngest brother, had a slightly malicious streak. The four eldest sisters were married and only occasionally at home. The youngest, very pretty, was adored by her father, and, as he said, just had to have a new dress every week! This brought

23

out my Puritan streak (no doubt tinged with envy) and while acknowledging the attraction of her gaiety and vivacity, it took me several years to appreciate her other good qualities. The middle sister, Sherin, after whom I eventually named my daughter, I came to admire and love dearly. She was warmly affectionate, and sensitive and intelligent enough to appreciate how I was feeling. She was also strong, with a core of steel, rather like John. As a group they had no conception of what life elsewhere, let alone in wartime England, could be like, nor any respect for John's and my educational levels. There was goodwill, but little common ground.

Racially segregated education

Our second problem would be the education of our children – in schools with Asian children only. I believed in one world. Growing up a Christian, I had, like so many other young people, quickly become disillusioned with orthodox religion. But the influence remained and I had always tried to live by the Christian ethic imbibed in childhood. I believed that all people were equal in the sight of God, and what was good enough for God, I felt, was good enough for me. Fundamentally, my sense of justice was deeply offended by the notion of rejecting other human beings just because their skins were darker than mine.

It seemed regrettable that my children should grow up knowing only little Indians, however delightful and intelligent they might be, but as John pointed out, he had survived those circumstances quite happily; and our family could, like him, eventually go to Britain for higher education. The problem seemed soluble – and was perhaps better viewed as a challenge.

However, it did not take long to realise that even that less-than-ideal scenario of our children going to John's old school, was untenable. His three young brothers, aged around 14 to 16 had all dropped out or were about to do so, without even attempting to sit O levels. They complained of poor teachers, and while they did not complain of poor discipline it was evident to us from their behaviour that we should find the school's standards unacceptable. They did no homework and their father viewed their scorn of education with benign indifference – as, apparently, did their teachers. This augured ill for K's grand design of a large family store, each department supervised by one of his sons. Circumstances since John's departure to England in 1936 had changed radically. Wartime contracts for tent-making and safari equipment for the military had made K a much richer man and, uneducated himself, he now blithely believed that money was enough, that he could buy his younger sons' paths to success. It could also be argued that he was now too busy to exert himself sufficiently to discipline them.

His taste for whiskey was now bankrolled and to our dismay he expected us to join him on his verandah of an evening while he indulged in increasingly maudlin accounts of his successful business deals and grandiloquent plans for the future of his family. Not only for his sons, but for his sons-in-law too. We found all this hard to take but a sense of duty kept us attending these sessions for several months.

Setting up in business

Then the bubble burst. Queries arose about some of those lucrative military contracts. This provided K's elder brother, Ahamed, a much wilier if utterly charmless man, an opportunity he had been waiting for, to ease his younger brother out of the family firm, Ahamed Brothers, replacing him with his own sons.

K was suspended from Ahamed Brothers, pending investigations. He became, understandably, morose, and the drinking increased. Tensions with John also increased. His father now had time on his hands to brood, and could not reconcile his need to dominate with John's independent attitude, developed and honed for over seven years in wartime England where he had had to make many difficult decisions entirely alone, and had survived magnificently, with high qualifications in pharmaceutical chemistry and in optics. Was K, I wondered, just a little jealous? They were both torn by conflicting emotions, and very unhappy.

Nevertheless, plans to set John and me up in business – the first brick in the planned family edifice – took shape. During the war few if any new buildings were erected in the colony. John and I had perhaps not fully appreciated our good fortune in finding a house, furnished and awaiting occupation, on the day we arrived in Nairobi, all thanks to his family. Vacant shop premises in Nairobi were non-existent. But, the NAAFI had recently vacated roomy premises in a building belonging to the dreaded Uncle Ahamed (alway referred to as Bapaji) situated centrally, close to the MacMillan Library. News was that he was renting it to the well-known firm of Dalgety, which planned postwar expansion. The suggestion was that John should beard Bapaji in Ahamed Brothers' shop, from which K was now banned, and petition him to ask Dalgety's to give up a corner of their large premises to be partitioned off as a small chemist's shop.

The brothers, Ahamed and Karmali Mohamed, had from their early years in Kenya (1911 to the early1920s) shared one house in River Road, with their wives and increasing families. Inevitably, tensions had arisen. Indeed it was the realisation that a future split between them was unavoidable which had inspired K to send his eldest son to England to become a chemist so that the family could branch out. There was no love lost between the brothers – though a superficial display of amity now existed. The community expected it and its appetite for scandal was so considerable that great efforts were made by all Ismailis to present an aura of equable amiability. This was what the Aga Khan impressed on his community, with considerable success. But hidden injustices sometimes festered away, eventually resulting in family break-ups in the next generation.

At first John baulked at his father's suggestion. He had no fear of his uncle but rebelled at the idea of asking him for favours. Were there any alternatives? None. So pride must be swallowed. The old man was less than gracious but agreed to think about it. K knew Dalgety's manager and did some behind the scenes lobbying, possibly over a whiskey or two. Agreement was reached and we began a hectic few months of planning and preparation.

Soon after our arrival in Nairobi in March I'd been approached by the manager of one of the two main chemists businesses in the town with the offer of a job as locum for three months while their regular pharmacist took war-delayed long leave. No way was I going to leave baby Jan. Why me, I asked? My husband is free to take the job. Somewhat reluctantly they agreed that that would be fine. They had, of course, wanted a European, not an Indian. Once there, John found everyone pleasant and agreeable and, one suspects, agreeably surprised to find him so congenial. It proved to be a useful opportunity for him to learn about local conditions, prior to opening our own business.

New Year's Day was a public holiday in Kenya and we spent January 1st 1947 putting the finishing touches to our little shop in Portal Street (now the Keswick Bookshop, selling religious literature). Half the space was dispensary and store, fitted to the ceiling with shelves; the other half, the shop, had walls lined with glass-doored shelves. At the back was a small room with lavatory and washbasin. And on January 2nd we opened shop. One counter was devoted to medicines, one to toiletries and a small one to photographic films.

By the time we had married the war had stripped most shops in Britain of even the most mundane items so most of our wedding presents had been in the form of cheques. Our little flat was very adequately equipped, we planned to leave England when war ended, so there was no immediate desire to spend our cash. It had taken me three years to repay from my salary the money I'd had to borrow from the Soroptimists and the Pioneer ladies and I had not married until those debts were discharged. So when John had suggested spending most of our nest-egg on a second-hand 35mm camera I had not demurred. It seemed an extravagance – but then, I loved the man. It proved to be one of the most rewarding investments he ever made

Meeting the Leakeys

Our second son, Peter, was born five weeks after we opened in business. This meant I could no longer take an active role and John did the dispensing as well as running the shop. In the dispensary he had the assistance of a locally trained African compounder, Julius, who worked only under supervision but was helpful in doing the heavier jobs.

A few months later I had a quite serious gastric attack, so our devoted Nandi ayah, Mariamu, took care of the children, aided and watched over by Ma and one of the sisters-in-law. More help came from an entirely unexpected quarter. The evening before I was due to leave Dr Thornton's nursing home, John brought news of a visit to the shop that morning from Dr Louis Leakey. Knowing we were scientists he had sought us out soon after our arrival in the colony and persuaded us to become members of the East Africa Natural History Society (EANHS), which is the oldest scientific society in Africa and which in the 1920s had established the National Museum in Nairobi, of which Louis was then curator. John had soon been roped in as a committee member and quickly became the society's treasurer. So we knew the Leakeys and indeed this was the foundation of our subsequent close association with the National Museums of Kenya. (Eventually, in the mid-1970s,

John became the first non-European chairman of the EANHS, a position he held for 14 years. When he retired he was elected the society's first patron.)

The news John brought that evening was that the Leakeys insisted I should not return home when discharged from hospital, but go and stay with them 'for at least a week'. In my weak condition I was moved to tears by this unsought gesture of kindness – from a Kenya European at that! Until then we had not appreciated what unique people the Leakeys were. They were entirely free of racial prejudice – Louis as an anthropologist knew there were no scientific grounds for considering one race 'superior' to another, a fact later confirmed by research in genetics – but your average settler was not about to change his views on such flimsy grounds as science.

So for the next week we and our two small sons lived with Mary, Louis, Jonny and Richard, together with innumerable Dalmations, in their tiny house in the museum grounds. Mary, utterly sweet, charming, and apparently unfazed by the doubling in size of her family, combined producing tempting meals with assistance to Louis in the museum and care of her beloved children and dogs. Richard, a shy two and a half year old, was only months older than our equally shy Jan. My main memories are of a shallow glass dish at the centre of the dining table containing floating verbena blossoms, Louis demonstrating his skill at fashioning various 'cat's cradles', learnt as a child from his Kikuyu playmates, the flight when dinner was over to reach a comfortable chair before a Dalmation exercised his prior right, and of Louis holding forth in fascinating scholarly mode after dinner, the glowing ash from his ever-present cigarette dropping slow, to Mary's despair, down the front of his khaki trousers, already well holed.

Feeling completely restored in strength and spirit, we returned to our Parklands bungalow at the end of the week, and thus to normal life. Ever since then the Leakeys have had a special place in our hearts.

At this time Jan was only two and Peter a baby. We still had time, but must begin to think seriously about how we should educate them, and do so in such a way as to give them maximum protection against prevailing European racist attitudes. They were good looking little boys, with skins a shade or two darker than mine. One thing we would never contemplate was to try to get them admitted to a European school. Even had we done so, their lives would have been intolerable, since the racial attitudes of Kenya society were already transmitted to its children, even at a relatively tender age.

A flying visit to England

By 1949 our business was reasonably well established and growing steadily. My health was improving but John felt a visit to Britain would do me good. Anticipation of this was already a tonic but the thought of the journey filled me with apprehension. I had never flown before, Jan was not quite four, Peter two and a quarter, or, as he announced to any enquirer, 'two and a porter'. This confusion had arisen from my descriptions of how they might find life in England rather different from Kenya, and where anyone who helped carry luggage was called a porter – not a 'boy'!

Flying in those days was less reliable than now and there had been some notable crashes, even of aircraft of reputable airlines. We flew in a South African Airways Skymaster and the journey was to take 25 hours, with refuelling stops at Khartoum and Tripoli. The worst scenario my imagination provided was of descending by parachute with a child under each arm. Airhostesses of that time were renowned for their beauty and hauteur, and those aboard our plane were no exception. I have no recollection of any helpful attention with my two little ones, and at one stage awoke to find one lolling, asleep, half off the next seat, and the other eventually discovered sleeping on the floor two rows ahead. That, of course, was Peter, the family comedian.

Landing at Khartoum alive and well not only converted me into a confident and seasoned traveller, but was a welcome break after five hours in the air. We dined in some luxury in an impressively smart hotel overlooking the Nile, the children being in surprisingly good form.

On to Tripoli, which was a misery. We hung around in a transit hut with inadequate and uncomfortable seating and, worst of all, only a pretty poisonous-tasting local Cola, and not much of that, to assuage our heat-induced thirst. But we survived, and eventually reached Heathrow (no walkways then, and its temporary-looking buildings appearing as if thrown up in a hurry) – and the arms of my family.

Six weeks later, restored and reinvigorated, we returned, courtesy of Air France, with three seats apiece to stretch out and sleep on, in very marked contrast to our outward flight.

Early friendships

After India gained Independence in August 1947 she set about appointing ambassadors to the rest of the world. Not until the following year did one arrive in Nairobi, and as Kenya belonged to the Commonwealth he was designated Indian High Commissioner, to East Africa, based in Nairobi. This was Shri Apa Pant, son of a rajah, an Oxford MA and barrister of the Inns of Court. His was a personal appointment by the prime minister of India, Pandit Jawaharlal Nehru, who emphasised to the Pants his deep concern about racial discrimination in South and East Africa, and urged them to build bridges of understanding and friendship between Africa's various communities.

Tall, handsome, and eloquent, Apa's exuberance and charm

concealed a deeply spiritual side of his character, which was the basis of his dedication to the concept of the brotherhood of man. He was married to Nalini, a statuesque, dignified and rather serious lady who, probably uniquely for an Indian woman of that time, was a Fellow of the Royal College of Surgeons. Kenya society had never seen anything quite like them. Apa – or Apasaheb to his compatriots, Apakaka to his children – was further remarkable in that he had persuaded his father, the old Rajah of Aundh, to comply with the Congress Party's desire (much resisted) that all Indian princes should in future renounce their titles. Apa himself would never be rajah. The Pants set about getting to know people of all races with energy and enthusiasm and we quickly became good friends.

They wished too to promote Indian culture, of which little was known in East Africa, even to many of those of Indian origin. Apa arranged for visits of prominent dance companies so that we learnt of the colourful varieties of Indian dance, kathakali, kathak, bharatnatyam, and were swept away by the brilliant spectacle of their subtle and precise beauty. In 1951, Apa was able to persuade Ravi Shankar, en route to England, to break his journey in Kenya. We went to one concert he gave at the Kenya Conservatoire and another at a private music party. Apart from the diplomatic corps, I recall few non-Indians availing themselves of such cultural treats. Apa Pant went on to become the Indian ambassador to a number of countries including Egypt, Italy and Britain.

In our early weeks in Nairobi John was delighted to be reunited with friends of his youth, known from school and mosque. Hassan and Gulie Rattansi lived quite near us in the Parklands area of Nairobi and lost no time in walking over and inviting us to dinner. Unusually, they shared their home with a Hindu bachelor friend of Hassan's, Dharam Kumar Sharda, always referred to as DK. As their families had lived upcountry (the Rattansis in Nyeri), they had been fellow boarders at the Government Indian Secondary School in Nairobi where their friendship was forged. At that time

DK could not afford to marry. A journalist with a sharp and self-deprecating wit, he was a most congenial companion and he and John felt an immediate rapport. This led a little later to John contributing a column to the weekly paper DK edited, rather on the lines of their beloved *New Statesman*, though not, it must be said, quite up to that standard. But it was good and, written in English, sold well within the Indian community. Hassan's young brother Piyo helped DK for a while on *The Tribune*, until in the early 1950s he left for Britain for further education. This opportunity Piyo pursued with such success that when he retired several years ago, it was as Professor of the History of Science at University College, London.

Eventually, quite unwittingly, DK was to contribute to the widening rift between John and his father. Taking a stroll in the garden one evening, K encountered DK approaching our verandah, where we happened to be sitting. They appeared from a distance to be having a short chat, then DK returned whence he came. A week or so later John called on DK and remarked on the fact that they had not met recently. It transpired that K had told DK that he did not consider him a suitable friend for his son, and had forbidden him access to our house. As John was then nearly 30, his reactions can be imagined. A blazing row ensued but though reassured, DK never risked coming to our house again.

Some wives, especially newly married ones, might have demurred at sharing their home with their husband's male friend. Not Gulie. She was an exceptional girl, pretty and fair, vivacious and self-confident, full of fun, and an excellent cook – a well brought up Ismaili girl in fact. This was not surprising as her wealthy father had, for his services to Ismaili causes, been made a count by the Aga Khan and was at that period his closest adviser in the community. Gulie had on several occasions travelled overseas with her father, learning to hold her own in any society.

Hassan's father was one of the first Ismaili pioneer immigrants in East Africa, travelling by oxcart some 400 miles from the coast to Nyeri near Mount Kenya in the early 1890s, where he established a grocery business. This was well patronised by local European farmers, and as with so many other Asian small businessmen in remote and isolated parts of the new colony, he helped subsidise them in the bad years of drought and animal diseases, which nevertheless bankrupted some of them. In this way many Asian immigrants wove a supportive economic web, without which more white settlers would have gone to the wall. They were able to do this by involving all members of the family, working all hours and living modestly. Mohamedali Rattansi, by the time I knew him, was a much respected elder of the community, a man of great character and determination. Even Gulie was a little in awe of him, even more so of his formidable wife Maniben. These qualities in Hassan were leavened by wit and humour, and the five of us spent many happy hours together.

In retirement and in gratitude for what they saw as their good fortune in life, Mohammedali and Maniben Rattansi set up a charitable educational trust to benefit each racial community in Kenya. Mohammedali's death, only months before inheritance tax would have been avoided, left Hassan with the well-nigh impossible task of accumulating sufficient wealth to ensure both the trust's and the family's future. He succeeded, and now, at the beginning of the 21st century, the Rattansi Educational Trust has made, and continues to make, an enormously significant contribution to Kenyan education and to the training of its badly needed craftsmen by providing bursaries to thousands of Kenya students, together with substantial grants to colleges such as Nairobi Polytechnic. For many years John was one of its most dedicated trustees. In 1998, in recognition of his work with the Trust, Hassan was awarded an honorary DLitt by the University of Nairobi.

My enjoyment of Ismaili friends was marred only by an occasional inability to understand what they were laughing at. When I asked anyone to explain, the invariable reply was that that particular joke would be killed by translation. One mistake I made was when, musing aloud about possible names for any daughter we may one day have, I asked 'How about "Jimijima"? I rather like that, it rolls off the tongue quite prettily.' John roared with laughter. 'That', he said, 'is not a name, it's what the family call Jimmy's mother, and that's what Jimijima means!' Oh well, I really did prefer 'Shereen'.

I'd always intended to learn John's mother tongue, to communicate with his family, but found when we reached Nairobi that all but his mother spoke fluent English. Furthermore, Kutchi, which they spoke among themselves more readily than English, was a dialect of Gujerati and could not be written. That fact coupled with my mainly visual memory, dealt a final blow to my good intentions. It also meant, sadly, that our children did not learn to speak an Indian language. Not for nothing do we use the term 'mother tongue'.

We made other Ismaili friends, most notably Madatali and Zubeida Thobani, who also lived nearby. Zubeida still ranks amongst my dearest friends. Until marrying Madat she had lived in Zanzibar, the third or fourth generation of her family to do so. Zanzibar had in previous centuries been the last staging post for captured Africans brought down from the interior and from whence they were shipped, mainly to America and Arabia. Zubeida's grandfather, Sir Tharia Topan, had been knighted by Queen Victoria for his part in abolishing this infamous slave-trade.

In the late 1940s and early 1950s, the British Government produced favourable schemes to encourage further white settlement in Kenya, which not unnaturally provoked deep resentment among the African population. Many of them had served overseas during the war as 'other ranks' in the Kenya African Rifles (the KAR) and had learnt not only that many other non-whites led better lives than they, but had also come into contact with what might be termed 'poor whites', in marked contrast to their own superior and often arrogant settler officers. This gave them food for thought. New settlement schemes which would deprive them of yet more of the land they considered their own, encouraged political unrest and contributed to the Mau Mau rebellion and eventual independence.

There were no barriers to entering and working in the country and many newcomers had broader, less prejudiced attitudes about race. Many, that is, when they first arrived, but quite a number of these readily succumbed to pressures to conform to the old-established ideas of European superiority. Others fortunately found this a ludicrous attitude and we began to find friends among them.

Religion

When discussing our children's future there had been one other area to explore: religion. Soon after coming to England John was befriended by the family of a fellow student, Jack Sims. Jack's father was a man of considerable character who had taken the difficult decision to be a conscientious objector at the beginning of the First World War and had suffered accordingly. A dedicated teacher and potential concert singer, he was also a confirmed socialist. Mrs Sims was a pianist, also potentially of concert standard, but barred from public performance by the handicap of delicate nerves. Musical evenings were a feature of the Sims's lifestyle and Mrs Sims played Beethoven, Mozart and Haydn, sometimes accompanying her husband's fine baritone.

John spent many vacations with the Sims. They were infinitely kind to him, and their standards and outlook on life had a profound influence on this rather callow youth, recently plunged into a strange new world. They also inspired in him a love of classical music which enriched his life and became central to the way he adapted to poor eyesight as he aged.

He began to question earlier assumptions. Always protective of his mother when his father had physically ill-treated her, he knew that she was helped through difficult times by her deep faith, and until leaving Kenya had himself regularly attended the mosque, or *jamaatkhana* (meeting house). Now he came to understand that non-Ismailis could also be decent and honest. Indeed, people need profess no religion at all, as in the case of the Sims, yet be disinterestedly kind. He would never again have a closed mind on religion, yet felt that for our children's sakes we should think of ourselves as Ismailis. That would mean my going to mosque. This disquieted me, but disillusion with Christianity, or rather, with those who supposedly practised it, led me to agree.

My sisters-in-law were dying to take me to mosque and show me off. Jan too must be taken as all children were, to be sprinkled with holy water. But my wartime wardrobe would let them down terribly. Laila's considerable collection of dresses was invaded and I was finally decked out in a crimson full-skirted dress, rather tight in the waist. My first visit to mosque was a fabulous experience. Instructed to leave my beautiful new suede sandals (no clothes coupons required!) in a heap at the bottom of the stairs, I rebelled. What if they were stolen? Never, they said, no-one ever steals things from the mosque.

Upstairs we went, and sat on the carpeted floor, everyone cross-legged. But after five minutes, cramp led to my rearranging my legs. Only women (plus Jan) were on this side of the hall, the men at the other end. Everyone, old and young, pressed forward to be introduced to me in the most friendly fashion and I greatly enjoyed the experience, though could understand not a word when the prayers began. And yes, when at the end we descended, there were my shoes, quite safe as promised.

Occasional attendance at mosque was not, it was explained to me, enough. I would have to be formally initiated, and as the Aga Khan would be in Nairobi in a few months time, after the Diamond Jubilee celebrations in Dar-es-Salaam, that's when it would be.

Came the day, and I was arrayed in a stunningly beautiful silver and white sari. John's father drove us to the Aga Khan's bungalow in Karen, Nairobi's most beautiful suburb. The Aga Khan was by then married to his fourth wife, the imposingly beautiful and statuesque Yvette Labrousse, now Begum Habibah Aga Khan. They received us most graciously, which slightly relieved my almost catatonic state of shyness. What a wise and kindly man this Aga Khan was. A Muslim who loved the West and had experience of its ways, he had an exact appreciation of the doubts and emotions which filled me. He assured me that as an Ismaili I should in no way be denying my Christian beliefs. Abraham (Ibrahim), Moses (Musa) and Jesus (Issa) were all prophets revered by Islam for their teachings about God's will. It was just that Mohamed, as the subsequent and last prophet, had revealed yet more of God's truth than the previous ones.

There was no formal initiation and after a chat over a cup of tea about John's experiences in Britain during the war, and of how the Aga hoped we might jointly contribute to the community's welfare, we departed, I in a relaxed and happy golden glow. In contrast to my shyness had been K's easy air of informality in the presence of his spiritual leader, which in some strange way increased my respect for him.

The history of HH Prince Sultan Mohamed Shah, Aga Khan III's, love affair with Europe and particularly with England, the Indian Imperial power, is long and complex. Suffice it to say that as a member of the Viceroy of India's Legislative Council, he had been involved in a plan with Lord Curzon, the then Viceroy, to settle in Africa many Muslims whose small farms in India had been devastated by drought. When, in 1905, he visited Zanzibar to arrange the settlement there of several hundred of his Indian Ismaili followers, he was appalled by the conditions he found. The African population had been weakened and debilitated by disease, notably tuberculosis, and was consequently lethargic and uninterested in work or progress or, indeed, religion. He saw that if his Ismailis were to be successful in the region their lives must be disciplined. He there and then set up a world-wide organisation for his communities, of territorial, provincial and local councils, which continue to this day. As well as concern for health, his other driving force was a passionate belief that education was the key to all success, together with a proper recognition of women's importance in society.

The Aga Khan Education Board

However, the incident which led to one of the most satisfying and intriguing of my Kenyan experiences involved Ismailis, and occurred in mid-1950. There was a tap at the door, and there were Madat and Zubie, with another man whom I'd once met at their house, Hadi Kothari. All Ismailis are deeply concerned with the welfare of their community. Hadi was no exception and had come up with what they all considered a brilliant idea. There was to be some reorganisation of local committees. Could they put my name forward to serve on the HH Aga Khan Provincial Education Board? I was simultaneously stunned and delighted, delighted to feel that they so clearly looked on me as one of them.

I did feel somewhat inadequate. Though better educated than most local Ismailis, any thoughts I may have had about education were based only on my own experience. But it would give me a chance to contribute something to the Ismaili community, as the Aga Khan had hoped. So, with my one eye, into the kingdom of the blind I blithely stepped, and began in mid-1950 to learn something about the inner workings of Ismaili administration. Several Nairobi schools were under us so I came to meet teachers and parents and listen to their problems. I also learnt how the local education system worked. It was run at that time by British colonial servants, many locally recruited, in the Department of

39

Education. The department was eventually raised to a ministry under Mr E.A. Vasey as its minister. My time on the board was utterly fascinating and rewarding, and I hope I also managed to contribute something .

The most intriguing insight was into the characters of some of the community leaders, especially when, a couple of years later, I was elected chairman of the Education Board and became, ex officio, a member of the Ismaili Provincial Council, the first European, to my knowledge, to be so honoured. How much I should have missed in life if fear of the unknown had held me back from that first visit to the *jamaatkhana*.

More about the Ismailis

Education Board meetings were held in what was then the main Ismaili mosque on the corner of Government and River Roads in the centre of the city. (Evening prayers were said upstairs in the main hall which extended over most of the area and next to it was the council chamber. The entire building was referred to as the *jamaatkhana*, or meeting place. People spoke of going to *khani*.)

The six or eight members of the Board met each month in a rather gloomy room on the ground floor. (Fortunately on these occasions I did not have to remove my shoes.) The chairman was Abdulrasul Kassim-Lakha, scion of a wealthy family based mainly in Uganda where they owned the best hotel in Kampala and a number of remunerative cotton processing plants. He wore a gold ring with a small diamond, which seemed to suggest that greater wealth could be called upon if necessary. Polished in manner, never seen without a rosebud in his buttonhole, he often exuded an air of faint amusement. But if I was ever a part of what amused him, I was confident that he was laughing with, not at me. I enjoyed his company.

The board had a secretary, Ibrahim Kara. Rather short, with a serious, composed expression and firm views, he received a small stipend, wrote all our deliberations down in rapid longhand and produced the longest and most detailed minutes I have ever encountered. By day he worked as a clerk in a lawyer's office which no doubt accounted for his insistence on meticulous detail.

When at subsequent meetings the minutes came up for confirmation Mr Ibrahim always put up strong resistance to any changes, any suggestion of error. If the chairman insisted, he would amend with reluctance and much shaking of the head. If that was what he had recorded, then that, he clearly felt, was what was said. It was a matter of honour. There were times in the future when we were indeed glad of such detailed records, a useful lesson, later, for me

Though quiet and generally uncommunicative, I came to see that as membership of the board changed with the years it was Mr Ibrahim's constancy and dedication to our work, to following correct procedures, which helped to weld us into an effective organism. In the early days I had harboured a faint suspicion that he did not entirely approve of this white woman coming in and attempting to run things. Yet Hazar Imam, in a firman to the *jamaat*, had praised me, and Hazar Imam's word was the word of God. Mr Ibrahim, I felt, was prepared to tolerate me. So when in 1957 I resigned from the board I was immensely touched when he sent me a personal letter speaking of my valuable advice and guidance, and predicting I should come to appreciate that I had made a great mistake in leaving the board. I certainly missed working with this kind, warm and congenial group of people.

Hadi Kothari, rugged of countenance, whose idea it had first been to involve me in the work of the board, was never lost for words. Though he came from a poor family he was now prosperous, yet inclined towards pessimism. Perhaps because of his early experiences he exhibited towards Mr Ibrahim (said to be the sole support of a widowed mother) a certain tenderness, a consideration for his real or imagined difficulties.

Amirali Karmali (no relation) was honorary secretary, which meant I suppose that he consulted with Mr Ibrahim as to how our correspondence should be phrased. Most of it was with the Education Department, some with the head teachers of our three schools, and occasional replies to an irate or vociferous parent. Amirali, quiet and amiable, eventually took over from me as chairman and I have no doubt was ameliorative and accom-modating to all.

Shamsu Nimji and Zubeida Thobani were other board members. We were joined after a couple of years by Habib Keshavjee, (Yusuf's father), newly arrived from South Africa. Originally Shamsu Nimji was our treasurer but he quickly brought in his brother-in-law Rahematali Abdulla to take care of our finances. Rahematali was short, portly and rotund, with a perpetual smile of contentment. Concerned not to overspend our finite resources, I would frequently consult him. 'Can we really afford that extra teacher in the nursery school, Rahematali?', or 'Are you sure finances will run to those new desks we so badly need?' He would beam at me. 'Why do you worry, madam chair? You should know I always see things are alright.' My anxieties would melt away. I thought the world of him. Occasionally, if a meeting ended early he would invite Zubie and me to a nearby hotel and press upon us what we then considered the most sophisticated of drinks, a Bristol Cream.

Zubie was my most trusted prop and stay. Such a stalwart character, wise in the ways of the community, she kept me on track if some of my ideas might be too unacceptable or offensive to some of the elders. She was young, intelligent, immensely practical, and understood the need to modernise.

At that time the community had two schools in Nairobi, the Aga Khan Girls' School, in a building which had been donated by the extremely wealthy Walji Hirji family and which my sisters-in-law had attended, and a recently opened nursery school, which owed its existence to the arrival in the city of Elizabeth Waeland, a young Austrian refugee who had trained under Anna Freud. Her parents managed a large sisal estate near Voi which belonged to the white pioneer E S Grogan. She began with a mere handful of tinies in a spare room in the girls' school. With a first-class training she also brought charm, humour, and warmth of personality, and her task was not only to guide the children in her care but to pass on her methods to several young Ismaili girls who had graduated through the big school and wished to teach.

The girls' school in those days took their pupils up to the London Matric. Some Ismaili teachers had had a little further training, but the advanced skills were provided by several expatriate women, and the headmistress was always an experienced European teacher and administrator, usually recruited locally. Quite soon the government opened a teacher-training college for Indian women at High Ridge in Parklands and this eventually provided a much needed supply of suitable and well-qualified teachers.

After a year or so Abdulrasul indicated that, because he would in future have to travel a great deal on business, he wished to resign from the board. To my surprise, he asked me if I would take over from him as chairman. Since the other board members seemed happy about this, I agreed. The job was certainly a challenge and one I could not have tackled without the support of my fellow board members. The chairmen of the various committees through which the community was led and guided were ex officio members of the Aga Khan Provincial Council, so I was truly elevated. What fun it was to sit and listen to the deliberations of leaders of the community, less so when I had to make my contribution. But they could not have been kinder or more helpful to me. Mrs John, they called me.

During part of this period John too was a member of the Provincial Council, under the chairmanship of his cousin Jimmy

Ahamed, who seemed grateful at times to draw on John's previous experience of committee work.

My whole time involved with Ismaili community work was personally rewarding and immensely enriching. The insight I gained into the way in which the community was organised, was a revelation. It began at the top with the Aga Khan, Sir Sultan Mohamed Shah, whose worldly – and no doubt spiritual – experience made him a figure not unlike the present queen of the United Kingdom, except that, unlike her, he held the reigns of power in his own hands. Also unlike her, although he had followers, he held no territory. He then delegated, down through the system he had set up at a meeting with community leaders in Zanzibar in the summer of 1905. This was a world-wide organisation of territorial, provincial, and local councils, whose leaders he would select from local candidates in each country. This network, with its subsidiary bodies, would deal with such matters as education, the care of widows and orphans, women's groups, funerals, and, in time, sports. A web was woven through which no Ismaili, affected by hard times, need fall. The Aga Khan shrewdly chose those in each locality whom he thought had the qualities of leadership. Then, with an occasional guiding *firman* read out in the mosques, he let them get on with it. On two occasions I was thrilled and indeed moved to be told of messages of appreciation for my work read out in the *jamaatkhana* from him.

Many of the community, my mother-in-law among them, looked on Hazar Imam, as he was known, as God. Their faith in him was immutable. Anything he asked of them, they would do, sure in the knowledge that they would benefit, certainly spiritually and almost as certainly, materially. Whatever the religion, it seems, faith is the *sine qua non*. Only through faith is one sustained. And it was, and is even more so today, an exceptionally successful and confident community. Now, I understand, the present Aga Khan is careful to avoid any suggestion that he is a god, portraying himself rather as a perhaps influential intermediary between Allah and his flock.

Above the Provincial Education Board was an education administrator, whose fief was the whole of Kenya. At that time the office was held by Ibrahim Nathoo, elder brother of Hassan, then Kenya's only Indian dentist, who practised in Nairobi. Both brothers had been among the founders of the Co-Racial school which had become Hospital Hill School, and Ibrahim had by now been nominated as a member of LegCo. A large, energetic man with a driving ambition, he had been chosen early in life by Hazar Imam, initially to serve the community, and then to be nominated to LegCo.

Ibrahim was a powerful man with rather thick sensual lips, who hugely enjoyed his power and the prestige it conferred. He once confided to my friend Hannah Vasey that he thought all men were more than averagely sexed, thereby demonstrating that an understanding of statistics was not among his many achievements. He was an extremely generous man and this trait seemed to be not only a means of gaining influence, but to stem truly from the heart.

Perhaps his main task was to encourage wealthy members of the community to provide funding for projects dear to the Aga Khan's heart, by identifying their spiritual leader's priorities. This would of course be quickly followed by consultations with the Aga Khan himself. The driving force of the development for which the Ismailis were generally so much admired was the desire to attract the blessings of their leader, given in extra measure in response to their generosity in promoting his plans for his people's welfare.

Accordingly, when I first became involved, the biggest plan afoot was to build a primary school to fill the gap between the nursery and the girls' secondary schools. This, as they said, would be 'mixed', a term I initially found ambiguous until told it would, unlike the high school, be co-educational. In one of the audiences John and I had with the Aga Khan in Paris I had asked, with my own small sons' future in mind, why he had founded a girls'

45

school yet nothing for the boys. As he explained, when you educate a woman you educate a family. Educating both boys and girls would have been the ideal, but funds had been limited when the Walji Hirjis offered the school building, and so he had plumped for educating the girls, while the boys continued in the government school with Indian youngsters of other faiths.

Now, an elderly Ismaili couple, the Rajans, came forward, offering the finance to His Highness for building the primary school. Coerced by Ibrahim, the government made available a large plot of land further along the Limuru Road beyond the girls' school, and building began. All this was under Ibrahim's jurisdiction and the provincial board had little to do with it at this stage. But in due course a magnificent modern building came into being, and our board was responsible for its staffing and management. Its official opening ceremony was conducted by the governor, Sir Evelyn Baring. Almost all the Ismaili community, and invited guests from all communities, were present. Many overseas pressmen, in Kenya to cover the emergency, came along too. Among them were the authors Philip Mason (who wrote under the pseudonym Philip Woodruffe), and Santha Rama Rao, whose books about India we had read and enjoyed.

Rivalry amongst Ismailis

Rather to his chagrin, another prominent Ismaili personality had had to take a back seat at the opening of the new school, which was dominated by Ibrahim Nathoo. This was Eboo Pirbhai, a small, compact, grey-haired man, much given to giggling. He had started out in life working for a taxi firm, soon graduating to owning his own vehicle and running a petrol station at the junction of River Road and Victoria (now Tom Mboya) Street, very close to the Ismaili mosque. In the 1930s, on his frequent visits to his

Kenya flock, the Aga Khan would avail himself of the services of Eboo and his taxi rather than bringing his own chauffeur. The illiterate, uneducated but wily Eboo lost no time in ingratiating himself with his spiritual leader and became indispensable. Steadily he rose through the ranks of the community and by the time we arrived in 1946 he was president of the Supreme Council of Kenya, a position of considerable power. His access to Hazar Imam was unlimited and immediate, and though superficially good friends, he and Ibrahim were quite clearly jealous of each other's positions.

We and our young Ismaili friends thought that before long Eboo would be ousted by the young lions training in Britain after the war in law and other professions. Gulie Rattansi's father, Count Jindani, a cultured man (I knew he was cultured because he would drink only Black Label whiskey!), had for many years been leader of the Kenyan community, but the Aga Khan had replaced him with Eboo. Gulie had witnessed Eboo's cunning in action and had no love for him. But he outwitted everyone and was eventually appointed by the Aga Khan as leader of all Ismailis, world-wide, which by then included Canada. No one could understand why he had such influence with Hazar Imam, especially when after the old man's death, his grandson Karim Aga, the new Imam, inherited and kept Eboo on until his death.

Eboo seemed to be almost universally disliked by fellow Ismailis. (Rumour had it that he and his wife had had some difficulty finding husbands for their daughters.) The eldest son, Badru, an ebullient and likeable personality, was being groomed by his father to take over from him, but tragically died at an early age. The next son, Ali, had no taste for power. After Eboo's death the young Aga Khan took steps to ensure that never again would such a position of influence in his community be held by a single individual.

Sadly, although Ibrahim Nathoo had contributed so much to the Ismaili community, especially in the field of education, his

47

high profile, high-flying, apparently successful career was to come to an unexpected end. He suddenly left the country, leaving his brother Hassan to sort out his affairs. Ibrahim died some months later in India of a heart attack, a tragic end for such a talented and able man.

Most of my work on the Education Board I greatly enjoyed, in particular the contacts with teachers, parents, and their everyday problems, some of which I was able to help solve. I loved some of these simple people whose lives were dominated by their faith and sense of service. Nevertheless, in time I became restless. There had been a little local difficulty over the community's, and therefore my fellow board members', unease about Ibrahim and the dashing blonde Scottish widow who by now was headmistress of one of our schools. I felt my position to be anomalous.

In 1955 a large conference on education was called by the Aga Khan in Cairo, of all education administrators and other senior office-holders and donors. Members of the community were all invited to submit suggestions and ideas they would like to be considered. By now the old man wintered each year in Egypt, and when he died in 1957 he was buried in an impressive mausoleum on an island near Aswan – which John and I visited with interest during a cruise of the Nile in 1987.

In my work in the community I had several times come across grief-stricken women who had been divorced, allowed to keep their children until the age of seven, but then had had to hand them over to the care of their ex-husbands, which in effect meant the care of his family. No doubt in many cases, hard though it was, the mother would be allowed reasonable access to her child, but in others she was not, and knew from neighbours how much the children pined for her, and often were physically and emotionally neglected. It seemed in many of these cases that, justified or not, a resentment against the mother poisoned the feelings of the father's family, and these feelings were taken out on the innocent child. Often there was an unsympathetic stepmother.

At the time, this had seemed to me an infamous custom, and I felt I could express my feelings – diplomatically of course – to Hazar Imam at the forthcoming conference. My brief letter outlining the possible iniquity of the system, was submitted through our administrator, who since Ibrahim's departure, was Jimmy Virjee. A lawyer about my own age, he was smooth, suave, polite and ambitious. Instinctively, I did not take to him on a personal level, but was confident that he would do a good job as administrator. In fact, the conference came and went and never at any time did I receive any acknowledgement that my humble submission had even reached Hazar Imam. The sting in this tale is that some 20 years later I discovered that the regulation about the children of divorcees is a basic tenet of Islam, laid down in the Koran.

They were kind to draw a veil over my ignorance, but could someone not have pointed this out to me? I could have been accused of not studying the Koran myself, but in fact the Ismaili sect does not refer to it in their daily lives, following instead the guidance of their Imam, who is of course steeped in its tenets. Aga Khan III (grandfather of the present incumbent) had followed its general principles but interpreted them in the way he thought best adapted for his community's life in modern times. Such is the practice of the mullahs and ayatollahs in other Muslim communities, not all of whom are such benign leaders.

A little while before leaving post in mid-1952, Kenya's governor, Sir Philip Mitchell, felt the time had come to accord recognition of the significant contribution the Asian community had made to the development of the three East African territories, in all of which he had served during his career as a colonial servant, and hence knew well. He suggested to the Colonial Office that each country should select an Asian candidate on whom a knighthood should be conferred. There was general agreement that such a gesture was long overdue. The governor of Uganda proposed Amarnath Maini, an eminent lawyer, that of Tanzania selected a member of the wealthy Karimjee family, and Philip Mitchell, we were later confidentially informed, was to nominate Ibrahim Nathoo. In the next honours list we read with amazement that, 'for his services to education', a knighthood was conferred on Eboo Pirbhai.

Not only was Eboo himself uneducated, but he had never made any contribution whatsoever to improving education in the community, which had been exclusively Ibrahim's domain. Surely, if the recipient were to be changed, so should the citation have been, to something more suitable? The community buzzed with gossip, and it was generally seen as yet another coup for Eboo and his influential relationship with the Aga Khan.

All this politicking in the community and particularly Eboo's role in it I found distasteful. Then there was the clear need of Mrs Walke's for more help at Hospital Hill, and the fact that when I took Jan and Peter to Britain, to help them settle in I was to stay away for six months. This, I concluded, was the right moment to resign from the education board. They gave me a wonderful farewell party and the Aga Khan conferred on me the title of Alijhani.

The school in the dining room

While I was in Britain in 1949 John had heard from Nalini Pant that in casual conversation at a recent diplomatic dinner party, she had garnered news of a young German girl who was likely to be seeking employment in the autumn as a governess. The Pants' daughter and son, Aditi and Aniket, were much of an age with our two boys, and they were as concerned as we about the problems of an adequate education for them in colonial Kenya. Nalini wondered if we would be interested in sharing the governess? Would we not! Nalini would find out more.

How wonderful, I thought – an answer to prayer, a blessing out of the blue! But, as I should have guessed, a long and arduous road lay ahead. Even so, Nalini's dinner party contact was the serendipitous encounter which would eventually lead to Kenya's first and highly successful multiracial school, Hospital Hill School. It was also, more modestly, the solution for many years to come of our worrying problems about the educational needs of our little family.

Nalini made contact with Thusnelda Welle, known always as Nelda, and discovered that she had been stranded in Uganda during the war, working as a governess in an American diplomatic family. They moved to Kenya at the war's end but were soon to return to the States. Already, nursery-age children of one or two English families in Nairobi were sharing her morning classes and Nalini arranged for her daughter Aditi and our Jan to join them for the remaining weeks of the term. But Nelda was looking for something more permanent. Her immediate family was located in what had become East Germany and she had no wish to go back there.

In my work with Ismaili schools, I had met Elizabeth Waeland, a brilliant young woman whose family were refugees from Austria and who, during the war, had trained in child education under Anna Freud in London. She was now headmistress of the Aga Khan Nursery School in Nairobi and on my visits there, we often chatted about the inadequate education available to young Asians in the colony. I had told her of our and the Pant's hopes of a private teacher and she mentioned an exceptionally bright boy in her class. Through Elisabeth, several other Ismaili families, thirsty for a better education for their young, heard of what we were doing and asked to join. At that time what was to become an excellent Aga Khan Primary school in the city was only in the planning stage, and would be for Ismailis only, with no international input.

So we had a teacher and a handful of pupils to share the expense of her salary – but nowhere to put them. Once again the Pant's involvement was vital. They too, as Asians, had been constrained by the iniquitous 'restriction' clauses in property deeds so could not live in Muthaiga, the 'smart' suburb of Nairobi where almost all other diplomats had homes. (The Indian government lodged a strong protest to the Colonial Office about this discriminatory practice and after several years, as Kenyan independence loomed, they were allowed to build an imposing mansion in Muthaiga for their representative, but this was long after the Pants, and several successive high commissioners had departed.)

Fortunately the Pant's house in Parklands, not far from ours, was large and capacious. As a temporary measure they offered their dining room each morning of the school week as a classroom. Each parent bought the necessary desks and chairs for their children – and we were on our way. This was towards the end of 1949.

Ideally, we needed a permanent home for the little school. Though we were all, including Nelda, passionate in our desire not to let the project fail, we needed time. It had not taken Nalini long to realise that her generous and impulsive gesture had created problems for Apa. The presence of a group of lively and occasionally noisy children was not an ideal accompaniment to diplomatic life, in particular official luncheon parties. From the beginning of the coming year, we must find some alternative accommodation.

We held a meeting of parents. We ourselves, with four other families (Kassam Kanji, Remu Verjee, Hassanali Gwaderi, and the Nathoo brothers), offered to find more money if it were necessary, and the search began for premises. Meanwhile it was time for our impulsive gesture.

Pre-war architecture in Nairobi was peculiar, or so we thought. The box appeared to have been its main inspiration. Our stone house had been built about 1928 and had front and back verandahs, the front one leading into the main living room, with a door off it to our bedroom on the right. Straight ahead from the front door was another one leading into a large hall, which had no fewer than a further seven doors opening from it. These led variously to the kitchen, some smaller bedrooms, a bathroom (no indoor lavatory), a store room, and the back verandah. This large hall we used as our dining room since it was of little use as anything else. Or was it? As a schoolroom, of course!

We heaved a collective sigh of relief, several other Ismaili parents asked to join in, with the realisation that they would be committed to paying a fee high enough to cover the teacher's salary, books and other equipment. Everything was going well, wasn't it? Then the blow fell.

Nelda, in great agitation, contacted us with the news that she had been served with a notice from the Kenya Immigration Department to leave the country within two weeks. As a non-British subject she had no right to residence and had previously worked in Kenya under a bond signed by her previous employer. After their departure it had eventually filtered through the bureaucracy that she was still, quite unlawfully, here. We were innocents in such matters and even the Pants had not appreciated the significance of Nelda's German nationality. One more problem, but we were determined to solve it.

Enter the Vaseys

A few months earlier John and I had met at a cocktail party the Mayor of Nairobi and his wife, Verry and Hannah Vasey. They were an interesting couple, much more relaxed and liberal in outlook than most local Europeans, and we had taken to each other.

Kenya owes much to Ernest Albert Vasey (always known as 'Verry'). An autodidact with a photographic memory, this illegitimate son of an itinerant actress first made his name in the 1930s as a Conservative in local government politics in Shrewsbury. He was also an accomplished actor. Coming to Kenya in 1937 he became involved in business in Nairobi, managed a cinema, and was soon elected (by a European electorate) to the town (later city) council. By the mid-1940s he was mayor of Nairobi and an elected member of the Legislative Council (always referred to colloquially as LegCo), his style and interests appealing to the local business community. Socially, however, he was less welcome to the 'establishment' because of his background. Married twice, both his wives were Jewish and this fact was held against him. Hannah, his second wife, became a good and supportive friend to me, insisting when the emergency erupted, that every morning, as the rest of us left for school and work, I leave Shereen and her ayah at their house with their son Michael and his nanny. The Vaseys lived nearer the city, an area considered less vulnerable than our own place out on the city's edge, adjoining the African reserve.

Hannah's parents had sent her to England in her teens but they and her younger sister had all been murdered by the Nazis at Auschwitz. A spirited individual, she managed to put the past behind her, and, unsurprisingly, was an ardent supporter of, and probably a marked influence on Verry's liberal views on race. The governor, Sir Philip Mitchell, thought so highly of him that he was soon appointed an official member of LegCo, crossing the floor, and being appointed first, Minister of Education and Local Government and later, during the emergency, Minister of Finance. He was made a KBE.

When in late 1952 Sir Evelyn Baring succeeded Mitchell as governor, one of his aide-de-camps was Charles Douglas Home, who later in life became editor of *The Times* newspaper. Charles wrote Baring's biography, in which he described Vasey as 'mouse-like', which seemed to those who knew him well as singularly inappropriate. Certainly he was small and quiet spoken. (I have occasionally been reminded of him by the Northern Ireland politician David Trimble). During the emergency Vasey in finance and Blundell in agriculture were probably the two ministers Baring (and therefore Douglas Home) saw most of, and in comparison to the bluff, florid, voluble, rather overbearing Blundell, Vasey may at first sight have appeared colourless. Blundell was adept at the art of self-promotion, something quite foreign to Vasey. On one occasion in the mid-1980s Blundell 'reminded' me that long before Independence, if we happened to be at the same gathering, cocktail parties and the like, he always made a point of coming to talk to John and me. Nothing could have been further from the truth. He was assiduously reinventing himself.

Verry Vasey, although quiet, could be forceful and was one of Kenya's most effective ministers, much respected in the City of London, where he succeeded in raising the finance which saved Kenya from bankruptcy during the emergency.

Sir Michael McWilliam, who in the 1950s served under Vasey in the Kenya treasury, found him at his most impressive at the despatch box in LegCo when he presented his annual budget. On these occasions Vasey's theatrical talents, acquired and honed in his youthful years as an actor, came into full play. It was, says McWilliam, a performance not to be missed.

Vasey's worth, together with his lack of colour prejudice, was eventually appreciated by some Asian industrialists, to whom he became not only a valued financial advisor who promoted the expansion of their business world-wide, but also an adoptive father figure to Manu Chandaria and his family, who supported and cared for him, both materially and emotionally, until his death.

When the problem about Nelda Welle's right to residence in Kenya arose, it was to Verry Vasey that we turned for advice. Appreciating our predicament, he promised to look into it. Derek Erskine was another LegCo member, whom we had not then met, though his reputation among the settler population for non-conformity and eccentricity – he was known locally as 'the old Etonian grocer' – had gone before him.

It so happened that Derek was chairman of the official

committee which considered appeals from foreigners to continue working in the country. The *sine qua non* was that an employer must sign a bond for such an individual, guaranteeing to pay their fare to their country of origin when, for whatever reason, their employment ended. With characteristic generosity, when told of the circumstances, Derek signed Thusnelda Welle's bond himself. It really began to feel as if the gods were on our side.

So in January 1950 classes began in our Parklands home, filled all morning with small scarlet and blue tables and chairs, which were rapidly stacked away as lunchtime approached. Conditions for Nelda must have been extremely difficult but she adored children and was a well trained and inspiring teacher who gave the appearance of enjoying her days every bit as much as did her small charges. There was, of course, a large garden in which they were periodically let loose to work off excess energy. Our cook and houseman viewed it all with tolerant amiability, dispensing fruit juice and other refreshments at break time. John and I were far from the fray, working in our chemist's shop in town.

Apart from providing the classroom, our responsibility was the financial one. John held the purse strings and kept the accounts, collecting and banking parents' fees, paying Nelda's salary from this school account, and issuing her with whatever the exchequer would run to for books, paper, pencils, etc. which she needed to run the school. All the while we were searching out a way to find more satisfactory permanent accommodation for the little school and a way to make it financially independent. With the move to the Pant's house and then our own the English parents had removed their children from Nelda's care so if her and our ideal of a truly international school were ever to be realised we must find a more suitable environment for it.

Unexpected help

Towards the end of 1949 we had been mildly surprised one morning to receive an invitation to dine at Government House. I had not followed the form for newly arrived Europeans in the colony to 'sign the book' so how did they know about us, we wondered? And if they did, surely they would wish to avoid us, pretend we weren't there, rather than to appear to recognise such an unconventional marriage? Perhaps, I speculated, Special Branch kept an eye on returning Asian students in case they had succumbed to Communist tendencies? Ridiculous, said John. A little later, a call from Verry Vasey made things clear. He had by now crossed the floor of the house, become an official member of LegCo and been made Member for Education.

It was a stroke of luck for us that Verry now had close and frequent contact with the governor, HE Sir Philip Mitchell, and in casual conversation one day had mentioned us and our concern with breaking down racial barriers, particularly in education. Sir Philip had expressed guarded interest, said he would like to meet us – and our invitation was the result.

My initial reaction had been one of mild panic because my wartime wardrobe had not included an evening dress. My sisters-in-law came to my rescue and decked me out in a discreetly coloured sari and blouse. I merely had to concentrate on not treading clumsily on the front pleats, so bringing the whole creation into a heap on the floor. I managed to avoid disaster.

The party that night was small and informal and included a delightful couple, the Maitland Edyes, who farmed up-country and were clearly close friends of the Mitchells. We immediately felt at ease and had a most entertaining and amusing evening. Government House was of imposing grandeur as was seen to befit Britain's imperial status. Its large, high-ceilinged rooms were connected by long corridors and furnished in suitably lavish style, with high windows opening on to wide, flower-bordered lawns.

John had been somewhat mystified when, after the ladies left the dinner table and the circulation of port and cigars had been observed, Philip Mitchell rose to his feet with the words, 'Let's visit Africa.' Through the French windows, out on to the lawn they trooped, stood in line – and watered the grass. Clearly this was a nightly ritual and, said Sir Philip, was why Government House lawn was the greenest in Nairobi.

Over drinks before dinner Sir Philip drew us aside from the other guests and asked us to tell him what we hoped to do. He was friendly and frank, and told us how deeply concerned he was about the country's racial divisions. He considered as we did that in the longer term these might well be healed by teaching children to live and play together before racial prejudice was established. But he warned us that he was trapped by the political realities of the moment and could never express these views openly. He added that while he could give us no overt help at this stage, he sympathised with our aims, and that if we could make our little school work for two years he would then give us whatever support he could, support as he put it 'for an experiment in multiracial education which had proved to be successful'. It was up to us to demonstrate that such success was possible.

Exhilaration at the prospect of help from such an unexpected quarter sent us home in a euphoric daze, convinced that failure was impossible. Such conviction was to be put to the test many times in the next few years, but Philip Mitchell had inspired us to feel that, quite apart from our own concerns, we had an added responsibility, never to let down a man of such unusual qualities.

That dinner also revealed to me something about myself. My whole attitude about living in a racial society had been totally positive. We would work towards reducing if not eliminating prejudice, but in the meantime I could manage very well without the friendship of whites. Yet how pleasant it had been to be in such congenial company and talking of common interests.

Sir Philip recorded in his diary that evening, 'Karmali and his

young English wife came to see me about their infant school . . .
I promised to arrange a meeting next week with Mortimer [C E
Mortimer, later Sir Charles Mortimer, then Member for Lands
and Local Government] . . . I said I was sure I could get help from
the Treasury at home.' Later, on 28th March, he wrote: 'At ten I
had a talk with Thornley, Mortimer and Miss Jenisch about the
possible high grade mixed infant school. Miss J. produced a lot of
pedantic educationalism in long words of little meaning, but the
others agreed that on the basis of what had been started by the
Karmalis we should surely be able to promote some sort of
development. We agreed to have another meeting with the
Karmalis . . . before I go on leave.'

The search for new premises

John had approached Nairobi's Town Clerk about the possibility
of erecting a 'temporary' building on a plot of land adjacent to
our house in Parklands which belonged to his father. K had been
very supportive about this idea and given it his blessing. These
were the days when Nairobi still had many wood and iron
buildings, some left over from the early part of the century but
still popular as they were cool to live in, easy to erect, and any
unsightliness readily disguised by colourful creepers such as
golden shower and bougainvillea.

But the Municipal Council was already looking forward to the
elevation of Nairobi to city status later in the year and doing their
best to eliminate 'low quality' housing. While not totally rejecting
the request, they might as well have done so. We were required to
sign an undertaking to remove any building at the expiration of
three months, or at any time thereafter at their behest. As we
needed an assurance of at least two years occupancy, it was just
not on.

59

Verging on despair, we turned to Sir Philip. He asked Charles Mortimer to give us discreet help. The Municipal Council's regulations could not be circumvented, but it did seem that if the buildings were erected on a piece of crown land, i.e. with a semblance of government blessing, no frivolous or unreasonable request would be made for its early demolition. K's plot was therefore abandoned and Charlie Mortimer and John began to cast around for a suitable and reasonably accessible piece of crown land.

At one time we almost shared Parklands Police Station plot (the officer-in-charge kindly gave his permission for Miss Welle to use his 'European sanitary accommodation') but this site was abandoned due to poor drainage, and was in any case scheduled for a new telephone exchange in the near future. The search continued for what felt an agonisingly long time, but Charlie was working quietly behind the scenes and on 14th August John received a letter from the City Engineer approving his plan to erect on Plot 57 Mpaka Road in Parklands, a 'Temporary Nursing (sic) School'.

Short, stocky, with florid complexion and a shock of white hair, Charles Mortimer epitomised the best kind of Christian. He never in my hearing spoke about his faith but certainly lived by the Christian ethic and was at heart ashamed of the racist behaviour of many of his fellow Christians. He once warned me, quite out of the blue, never to attempt to attend a service at All Saints Cathedral in the city, where he and his wife worshipped. 'They would give you a very hard time, Joan,' he said. Fortunately I had no illusions about Kenya's white churchgoers.

Mortimer tried in other ways to influence Kenya Europeans to become more tolerant of the other races among whom they spent their lives. When in 1958 John was eventually elected to Nairobi Rotary Club, he, his cousin Shamsu (Sammy) Ahamed and a prominent Sikh, Kirpal Singh Sagoo, were the first non-Europeans to dilute the previously entirely white membership, in spite of such intolerance being the very antithesis of the spirit of Rotary. He then learnt that for several years Charles Mortimer had been supporting the efforts of Vic Browse, the colony's foremost optician, in putting John's name up for election, only for it to be blackballed. When the three Indians were elected, one long-standing member resigned in protest. He retired in due course to what was clearly his spiritual home, South Africa.

Charlie was a friend of John's father. K's high profile as Ahamed Brothers' front-of-shop salesman, a task at which he excelled, had made him a number of friends among the Europeans who patronised the store. In addition to the tent-making which had been Ahamed Brothers' original raison d'etre, they were now well known for their tailoring skills. Leading colonial servants, politicians and of course up-country settlers (Beryl Markham among others) were all numbered among their customers and the ultimate accolade awarded them was permission to display the Prince of Wales's feathers and 'By Appointment to the Prince of Wales' on their letterheads and wrapping paper after they kitted him out for his safaris during his visit to Kenya in the 1920s.

Ahameds employed some 40 tailors and tentmakers, mostly Goans. Goans are Roman Catholic and rather than get their tongues round the difficult Ismaili names of the Ahamed and Karmali children who in those early days played around their feet, they endowed them with Christian names. John became John instead of Shamsudin, his two elder Ahamed cousins were Jimmy (Badrudin) and Tommy (Sultanali). In time only their mothers used their Ismaili names.

While all these lengthy negotiations about a suitable plot were going on, Nelda, in spite of a full day's teaching, had not been idle She had located an ex-army hut out at Thika, setting of Elspeth Huxley's *Flame Trees of Thika*, which she felt could be usefully adapted to her purpose, and was reasonably priced. After a happy day's outing with the children to view it, it was purchased, dismantled, and transported by lorry, with help from a friend of Nelda's, the 30 miles to our Parklands site.

We had called a meeting of parents and Nelda. Five families (Kassam Kanji, Remu Verjee, Hassanali Gwaderi, the brothers Hassan and Ibrahim Nathoo and ourselves) volunteered to contribute £50 apiece. The resulting £250 was sufficient to cover the cost of the hut and its transportation, leaving a little over for extras.

In granting John a temporary occupation licence for the school the city council had, of course, insisted on being shown 'satisfactory plans'. These were drawn up, generously without charge, by a young Hindu architect, Chandra Thakore, whose children were later to join the school, and had included a necessary concrete toilet block adjacent to the hut. Nelda employed casual labour to cut the long grass, providing a playing field of an acre or two, and in a few months swings and a sandpit were in place.

Kenya's two annual rainy seasons mean that trees and other plants grow at twice the rate of those in more temperate climes. In no time at all the rather ugly sanitary block was disguised by golden shower, crimson bougainvillea, and eye-achingly blue morning glory, so that, together with a colourful flower border, the school looked attractive and as if it had been there for ever. In large letters on the schoolroom wall Nelda had painted a motto in Esperanto. Its translation into English read, 'Let us serve in honesty, integrity and love.' She was motivated in her dedication to the school, as she later recorded, by 'a deep desire that further generations should regard differences in society as assets rather than dividing agents'.

Clearly, there were whites, albeit very few, who were less than happy with Kenya's racial set-up. For the most part they were rather ordinary people, not in positions of power, and if of Christian conviction finding it uncomfortable to practice all its precepts in such a society, but ready to help in unobtrusive ways. From among these Nelda found support, including one who 'taught for a whole term without remuneration'. We knew nothing of this then as Nelda was not communicative other than on financial matters, but think it may have been Grace Bartlett.

Early in 1951, our dining room was vacated and the new school year began in the hut at Mpaka Road. But goodness me, how was it to be identified? That small matter had quite escaped our notice till Nelda pointed it out. 'How about Co-Racial School?', she asked. It seemed a bit clumsy, but had the virtue of accuracy. That agreed, we sat back and relaxed – which, as always in this story, was a mistake.

The need for a multiracial school

But it did mean an opportunity to take stock. As we had told Sir Philip, our ultimate aim was to make our school international by attracting African parents to enrol their children. With some permanence to offer and in such pleasant surroundings, Nelda and Nalini felt it should not be too difficult to find new European pupils and this indeed proved so. Quite soon our enrolment went up to 15 pupils, which was about as much as could be coped with by one teacher, and children ranging in age from four to six years.

Finding African pupils was a different problem, and one we would postpone until we could demonstrate that mixing just two races worked well. In that immediate post-war period there were in fact few if any African parents in Nairobi who could afford to pay even modest fees. There were several government schools for Africans on the city's outskirts, and there, of course, lay the rub. Education in the country running on totally racial lines was bad enough in itself, reinforcing as it did the racial divide. But the sums of money allocated to each community were heavily biased. The annual sums per primary day school pupil in the year 1959 (the only year for which I have a record, but it is representative) were £85.17 for Europeans; £28.12 for Asian; and £2.07 for Africans. The educational standards achieved by each race almost precisely reflected those differences.

When tackled about this differentiation, any colonial servant – and certainly any settler – would point out that there were far more African than Asian children to be educated, and relatively few European, so it was a just allocation of available funds overall. They added that it was the European population which paid most in taxes. There was truth in this, but nevertheless the policy was unfair and short-sighted.

The rite of passage to secondary education, the Kenya Preliminary Examinations (KPE) were similarly different, their standards descending as one would expect. Again, the defence by the authorities was based, not on their belief that non-European races were incapable of higher learning and so should be denied access to it, but because of 'the difference in cultures'.

Settler sentiment governed life strongly. LegCo in those days consisted of unofficial (elected) European members, official European members appointed by the governor (presumably in consultation with the Colonial Office), one or two nominated Indian members, and a nominated African.

Some colonial servants were dedicated to Britain's commitment to run her colonies in the best interests of the local inhabitants, 'the natives', but the majority, many of whom were by then locally recruited, took the settler viewpoint. It was in this atmosphere that Sir Philip had to operate. If he took too strong a line with the settlers in trying to impose his own more liberal views, they could threaten – as they eventually did over another issue – to march on Government House.

A humane man of broad vision with wide experience of Africa, Philip Mitchell had previously been acting governor of Tanganyika and then governor of Uganda. While secretary for native affairs in Tanganyika he had once confided to his diary his fear that 'all my work' will be undone, [so that they can] 'start the miserable Kenya methods here'. But he was now in Kenya where settlers pre-dominated and were extremely vocal, so pragmatism was the order of the day.

Asian communities had begun to set up their own schools, witness the Aga Khan schools with which I had become involved. The plot the Co-Racial School occupied in Mpaka Road was designated in the city's long-term planning as the site of a school for the Hindu Visha Oswal community. African aspirations for better education for their children were addressed by the missionaries, mainly Roman Catholic and Presbyterian, this latter being largely run and funded by the Scottish kirk. These schools, most notably the Alliance High School at Kikuyu (given that title because several Protestant denominations had collaborated in establishing it) and Mangu High School run by the Catholics (although there were many others), provided first class education for a select few promising African boys, quite often the sons of chiefs.

Other Africans either worked on the land, their own or more usually on white-owned farms and ranches, or as domestic servants. A very few were employed in minor clerical jobs or as messengers and the like, in business organisations in the towns. None of them at that time earned enough to pay for private education for their offspring. But that was soon to change. A number of African young men progressed through the top class mission schools and were to find better paid jobs. Some even managed to get overseas to university, a process not encouraged at that time by the Colonial Office. In South Africa Fort Hare's students were non-European and, of course, British universities were open to all who could pay and reached their required standards of entry.

When in the late 1940s and early1950s we had met and made friends with several recently arrived British couples who suffered from no racial prejudices, we had found this very refreshing. What was also true was that when in 1947 it became clear that

65

Indian independence was imminent, other new white arrivals in Kenya were perhaps even more prejudiced than old residents. These were the 'last-ditchers'. As in due course Kenya began to change, they moved on to what was then Southern Rhodesia and eventually when that country began in their eyes to 'deteriorate', to South Africa. But Kenya was a very comfortable ditch for them for a good many years. Mostly from India, often ex-army, they were authoritative, assertive and vocal, more eloquent than the early settlers, many of whom just wanted to get on with their farming and be left alone. Every liberal measure suggested in LegCo or the city council met with vociferous opposition. We knew, and so did Sir Philip, that sooner or later our mixed-race school would come to their knowledge and the battle would be on. Softly, softly, must be our motto.

Looking back it appears to us that those Africans who were conscious of the inadequacy of the education offered to their children in colonial times were, rightly, more immediately concerned with initiating political change. In this way they were to gain the power which would enable them to implement economic, social and educational changes. In short, in the first five years or so after the war, there were few if any Africans with children of early primary school age who had both an overwhelming desire for them to achieve a better standard of schooling and the economic resources to pay for it. If such an African parent had approached us, he would certainly have been warmly welcomed.

The most frequently voiced opposition to a school such as ours, in itself a facet of racial prejudice, would be that by mixing the various races educational standards would fall. Our intention had always been to provide an education which was at least as good as, if not better than, any school in the country. In the circumstances of the day that meant the academic standards of the European schools. The second criterion to be met if the few 'colour-blind' parents were to be attracted, was that the cost to them should be no higher than that of their own schools. This was readily implemented by fixing the fee for a European child at that level, at the time £5 per term. In its early years, Asian parents paid £8 per term, and often supplemented this with gifts towards obtaining extra equipment.

All school expenses, the highest of which was the teacher's salary, had to be met from fees, and Nelda too made personal sacrifices. A memo from the acting director of education, dated May 1951, says 'Miss Welle now gets £25 per month but is said to use £10 of this on school expenses.'

The first board of governors

For some time John had been aware that running a school was not a single-handed task and had been looking around for others who might be sympathetic to the aims of this one. He needed people who had something to contribute and who would share his responsibility.

We had been encouraged to realise that we were not alone in desiring to improve race relations in Kenya. As we were later to learn, less than a year after we arrived in Nairobi the United Kenya Club had been formed. 'It's purpose', to quote Tom Askwith, one of the club's founders, in his immensely informative book on the life of an official working in immediate postwar Kenya, *From Mau Mau to Harambee*, was 'to provide a meeting place for those of goodwill and free of racial prejudice on a basis of complete equality . . .' In due course, we were elected to membership. One got to know other members of all three races at the club's weekly lunches – which cost just one shilling. There we made not only new friends but what were to prove useful and rewarding contacts.

In mid-1947, as a result of consultations between the governor,

Sir Philip Mitchell, and Arthur Creech Jones, the Labour govern-ment's Secretary of State for the Colonies, the first representative of the British Council arrived in Kenya. This was Richard Frost, a graduate of Oxford and Harvard and an experienced journalist. Even more importantly, he was entirely committed to his brief, which was to improve race relations in the country (seen by Creech Jones as 'an urgent need'), specifically by establishing an institute 'to provide cultural facilities and promote inter-racial under-standing'. In other words it was, like the United Kenya Club, to steer clear of any political involvement. Dick Frost was an early member of the club. (His book *Race Against Time* and his later biography, *Enigmatic Proconsul: Sir Philip Mitchell and the Twilight of Empire*, provide a wealth of material on the Kenya of that time and from which I have several times quoted.)

Another UKC member was E J Clarke, a teacher who was a provincial education officer in the Education Department. John approached both Dick Frost and Ted Clarke, inviting them to become, with him, members of an unofficial board of governors of our school. In addition, the Reverend W. Scott Dickson, then general secretary of the Christian Council of Kenya, and Ibrahim Nathoo, who with his brother Hassan had been one of the original contributors to the school's founding funds and could be a useful adviser to it in his capacity as a member of the Legislative Council, were invited to join the unofficial group. All accepted, but their first meeting, scheduled for 19th February 1951 in the British Council offices, appears not to have taken place.

Not until 13th June is there a record of any meeting, and the one which then took place 'elected Mr Karmali as Chairman of the Board of Governors which was in process of formation'. The minutes occupy a single foolscap page and reading them through leaves one with the impression that the future of the school was bright indeed. Through Mr Vasey, £8,000 was being offered from 'an outside source' and this 'might be matched by a similar amount from the Development and Reconstruction Authority (DARA) to provide permanent buildings on a site which had been promised by Government.'

A faint note of doubt did creep in when 'Mr Karmali explained that . . .negotiations which Mr Wadley was conducting within the Education Department seemed to have been delayed.' It was a pattern which was to recur again and again, high hopes being engendered only to be gradually eroded or bogged down by lack of interest or unvoiced opposition within the Education Department. We were innocents abroad, unable at that stage to comprehend the wiliness of civil servants determined to undermine or sidetrack policies with which, for personal reasons, they disagreed.

And what of W J Wadley, the then Director of Education, who was to attend future meetings of the board of governors as the department's representative? And should, surely, represent the school's interests to the department? A difficult assessment, but we were inclined to give him the benefit of the doubt and conclude that he was, albeit cautiously, favourably inclined. Within his brief at that time the Co-Racial School was indeed a small and minor matter, and many of the delays were no doubt due to pressure of other work, but it is equally certain that some of his colleagues in the department were actively opposed to the idea of multiracial education and indulged in quiet acts of sabotage or deliberate neglect. Perhaps Wadley was just a cautious and correct civil servant.

There was that other factor, apparent to me, more attuned as I was than John to British attitudes, that we were that deplorable thing, 'a mixed marriage', and, ipso facto, generally immoral, unsuitable people to dabble in the sacred waters of education. They were also unaccustomed to the confident and assertive manner of John, someone who, in their lexicon, belonged to 'the lesser breeds without the law', and should know his place.

Nelda meanwhile wrestled with her problems, the most niggling of which was the 'illegal squatter', still living in his small hut and growing maize in the school grounds. In mid-February she wrote to John plaintively complaining that '. . . when we tried to terrace last week he got wildly excited again'. Not wishing to quarrel with him and distress the children she had sent a series of notes to Parklands Police Station, as a result of which 'the man is arrested for ten days . . . During the weekend however, he has pulled out a number of trees we had planted and threatened to destroy the rest of our garden.'

Could some authority be invoked to remove him, his hut, and his belongings? 'For now he is becoming unpleasant.' In June he erected yet another hut. In September he had harvested his crop, so could he not now be induced to move? His last appearance was towards the end of November, when the town clerk contracted to perform yet another demolition but added sadly that 'the Council has no bye-law which empowers it to cause [this person's] removal.' Thereafter the squatter is lost to the record, so that one assumes he accepted defeat and moved on to squat elsewhere, leaving a picture in microcosm of a problem typical of rural Kenya of the time.

In this case the plot of open land on which the school stood could have comfortably accommodated both the squatter and the children, but unfortunately his resentment of the school's intrusion on what had seemed to be his own domain had made him aggressive and difficult, and so he had to go.

Our growing family

Otherwise things seemed to be going well. Certainly our two boys could hardly wait to set off each morning, accompanied by Mariamu, our ayah, to walk the half mile or so to school. Home for lunch with us, a rest on their beds with a book, then another walk with Mariamu or playing in the spacious garden equipped with natural 'climbing frames', frangipangi trees and the like.

The lower garden on K's plot had once been planted with citrus trees but years of neglect even before he moved there meant the crop was negligible. Near our house, however, were two abundantly fruiting trees, a guava and a locquat, or Japanese plum. To my everlasting amazement, the boys adored unripe guavas, really hard green ones. 'Collywobbles!' I warned. But strangely these never developed and to this day the only apples they will eat are those which are green and hard.

August 1951 saw the final addition to our family with the birth of our daughter, Shereen. A month before her arrival I stopped working, and when she was old enough to be left with Mariamu – and I could just bear to do so – I was able to work mornings only. The knowledge that Ma, blind though she was, lived only 20 or so yards away from our house, was reassuring when I just had to help John develop our business by undertaking the dispensing, stock control, and generally helping in the shop. In 1949 Ellis Monks, then the government pharmacist, joined us prior to setting up his own business as a chemist specialising in veterinary medicines. He had had the tremendous good fortune of serving his apprenticeship in a business which did just that. His specialised knowledge was invaluable to settler farmers whose stock diseases were numerous, varied and often difficult to contain.

Our business, in which K and his younger sons had shares, was registered as J S Karmali Ltd., and we now set up in the same modest premises a joint company, Monks and Karmali, to deal with veterinary medicine. The idea was that while doing our dispensing when I was not there, Ellis would develop the veterinary side until such time that it could be self-supporting, when he and the company would move out to other premises. His wife, Peggy, a nurse, was a valuable addition to our staff. In the event in late 1952 our own show, now with a thriving photographic side, moved out into much larger premises in Hardinge (now Kimathi) Street, leaving the Monks's *in situ* until, several years

71

later, they too sought larger premises, and we eventually dissolved the partnership.

I mention Shereen's birth casually, *en passant*, but the circumstances surrounding it serve vividly to illustrate the depth of the prevailing colonialist prejudices. Long before, having seen conditions for myself I had, pragmatically, abandoned in two respects my intention to use no facilities in Kenya which would be denied to John. First, since Asian educational and medical institutions were inferior, I had determined to use European hospitals should the need arise. It would, I felt, be foolish to jeopardise my health when so much depended on me. I was persuaded into the second change of heart by the English librarian of the MacMillan Library, a delightful man called Kemp, who urged me to join it, which as a European I could, and so borrow books which not only I but John too could read. It worked wonderfully well – Mr Kemp later told us that the request lists which we put in each month were of the greatest help to him in compiling his book orders. One hoped that Mr Northrop MacMillan, whose bequest had founded the library, stipulating that only whites should use it, was not spinning too dizzily in his grave.

But to revert to hospitals. Dr Gregory, an Irishman and prominent Nairobi medic, was my doctor when I was having Peter, and he without a qualm booked me into the Maia Carberry nursing home for my confinement. Though this was strictly 'Europeans only' the matron (Joan Heycock) and her staff were all quite charming to me, and I was visited each day by K as well as John without any comment or restriction. By the time of Shereen's advent, gynoecological and obstetric patients had a new and well equipped hospital, the Princess Elizabeth, again for Europeans only, and into this my new doctor, the much loved Guy Johnson, arranged for me to be confined when the time came. In each case, of course, quite rightly, we paid full fees.

There had been a great drive to raise funds for the new hospital and all prominent firms in the city, including J S Karmali Limited, had been canvassed to contribute, which we had been happy to do.

Above our little shop in Portal Street were two medical practices, one of general practitioners (William Boyle, Guy Johnson, Digby Flowerdew and Mary Harris) and Arthur Pullar, an ophthalmologist sharing consulting rooms with William Powell, an ENT man. Powell's wife, Edna, also a doctor, seemed to dabble in obstetrics but was not much in evidence.

It transpired that a couple of months before my baby was due, Edna Powell and Mary Harris had been in the office of the matron, at the Princess Elizabeth hospital, presumably checking on projected dates for their own patients' deliveries, when the eye of one of them was caught by my name. They reported this fact to the East African Womens' League, which had raised money towards equipping the hospital, and this organisation gave them full support in their attempt to have my booking cancelled. When it was pointed out to these ladies that I was in fact European, they countered with, 'Ah yes, but the child she produces will be half Asian'.

Guy Johnson was scandalised by this slur on the standards of medical ethics and referred the matter to the hospital board. And there, to their eternal credit, I had my champions, notably Betsy Woodley whose husband was the current mayor of Nairobi, and the Very Reverend David Steel, pastor of St Andrew's Scottish Presbyterian church (not to be confused with his more famous son, onetime Liberal Democrat MP, now Sir David Steel and presiding officer of the Scottish Parliament). Just what was said to the two women doctors we never knew, but John was quickly told that of course I should be admitted when the time came. Once again, I could not have been better looked after, and indeed the nursing staff seemed if anything, by their kindness and attention, to be trying to make up for the behaviour of Drs Harris and Powell. But I am glad I knew nothing of the furore about my admission until long afterwards. Only later did John tell me that while Harris and Powell had been trying to exclude me, he had

73

gone to the fundraisers and said that if his child was not good enough to be born in the hospital, he felt his money might also contaminate them and it would be best if it were refunded. Neither of us can now recall what their response was.

Like so many mothers of the generations following mine, I grappled with my conscience over the tussle between career and childcare. In this case it was more than 'career', it was our future livelihood. John could not run the business alone, entailing as it did an increasingly busy dispensing schedule and the fast developing photographic section in which we faced less competition from the two large and old-established chemists shops in the city. It was an immense relief when I was able to work only in the mornings. It also enabled me to follow up school concerns for which John was too busy, and report back to him. We still awaited more positive news from the Education Department but otherwise things seemed to be going well.

Finding another teacher and securing funding

The bombshell fell on 18th July 1951 when Nelda wrote to John informing him that she was to be married in three weeks time, and so 'would not be available for the school much longer'. She continued, 'I've made great efforts to get suitable teaching staff with the result that I have two teachers in view in England who would be prepared to make this school their immediate object if I could make them an offer of a reasonable salary.' One of them, 'Miss P', was a Kenya girl, Froebel-trained, and would be available next term. 'I am particularly anxious,' she added, 'to get as head of the school a person with a sense of mission, and not just someone who would like to earn some money by teaching.' After a few further suggestions about the school she concluded by asking for a quick decision from the board on what salaries she might offer the new teachers, and in a dither of indecision, perhaps induced by knowledge of the consternation her letter would provoke, signed herself 'Yours faithfully, T M J Welle' and 'Yours sincerely, Nelda'.

A few days earlier Wadley had sent a memo to his minister, Mr Vasey, on the 'Inter-Racial Kindergarten School', discussing its finances for 1951–52 and pointing out that there were no 'grant-in-aid' rules under which it could be assisted. 'I have assumed', he wrote, 'an ad hoc decision will be made to assist this particular case.' In provisional estimates for 1952 he had allowed £750, 'though more grant may be needed if the school proved such a success that it became necessary to employ extra staff'.

But in a letter to John next day he seems to have drawn back several paces. 'I must point out that the figures on the attached paper (Estimates for 1951) were only tentative ones and I have since had to reduce them *in the light of the existing circumstances* [my italics] . . . but I should like you to know that the matter has been under continuous consideration.' Bearing in mind that the figures mentioned in his memo to his minister for shortfalls in 1951 and 1952 (£650 and £750) were a minute fraction of the budget for European primary schools at the time, it did appear that other factors besides money were influencing the department. At the end of July Nelda wrote a 'winding up' letter to John in which she thanked him 'for having done all the tiresome business side which I could never have tackled'.

The remaining months of 1951 were ones of deep frustration for us and everyone concerned for the school's future. 'The light of the existing circumstances' quoted by Wadley was a sinister one, casting little helpful illumination on the actions of European officials in the Education Department. The prominent men on the board of governors were involved in other affairs. In a letter early in August John told Scott Dickson that 'Mr Frost is away and will not be back until the end of August. Mr Ibrahim Nathoo is also likely to be away so an immediate meeting would be reduced to the three people who are already in the know, which would serve no useful purpose.'

Scott Dickson, the most committed of the new school governors, who was sadly soon to be lost to the board through ill health, wrote to a Mr L B Greaves in London stating, *inter alia,* that 'the Froebel Institute in London is interested and is I understand willing to provide some capital for a new building and help recruit staff. On behalf of the governors and with the consent of Wadley, the Director of Education and Vasey the Member for Education etc I have been asked to write to you and request that the A.G.H.S vetting committee meets and vets a Miss P., with whom Miss Welle has been in contact.'

By mid-September, frustrated by a situation in which chances appeared to be slipping away because of the board's inability to meet, John acted, writing personally to the director of the Froebel Institute. After setting out the facts about the school he concluded, pointing out the urgency of the matter, 'I am anxious that this experiment, the first of its kind in Kenya, which has cost much sacrifice for several years, should not come to an end for lack of suitable staff.' To this letter he received a helpful and courteous reply, dated 27th September, from the secretary of the National Froebel Institute saying they had an agency for teachers, and 'we will willingly do our best to help you'. After asking for details of any contract offered, he concluded, 'We are very interested to hear of the foundation of an inter-racial school in Kenya and if you could we would like to see a prospectus.'

The final act in this mini-drama came, as Scott Dickson related, '. . . an impossible muddle over Miss P and I fear that Miss Jenisch has been partially responsible. Neither Mr Beare nor Miss Jenisch has been the least bit helpful.' Miss P, arriving a month earlier, had been told in the department that 'there was nothing for her, and eventually a job had been found for her in a school in Kericho'.

Miss Jenisch appeared to be totally opposed to the principles of the school, as suggested by Philip Mitchell's comments at an earlier stage about her lack of enthusiasm. Unfortunately for us she was strategically placed, in a senior position in the Education Department, to covertly derail our progress. She had strong South African connections and had never, to our knowledge, exhibited any positive attitude to the idea of multiracial education. In fact a number of things were going on behind the scenes of which we had no knowledge.

During all this ineptitude and subversion, Mrs Kroll, as Nelda now was, had returned from Molo where her husband was an agricultural officer, to keep things going while efforts to ensure the school's survival continued. Nelda was near despair and wrote John a long, rambling and passionately concerned letter, commenting on the slackness of the Education Department in answering letters and the apparent 'ill-will somewhere at Mr Wadley's . . .'. She rightly said that she could not continue after this term and that if a teacher could not be found, the school was doomed. She and we cast around in desperation for a locally based teacher. A Mrs Grace Bartlett expressed interest and was shown round by Nelda, but turned the post down.

We heard from Verry Vasey, the Member for Education, that as far as he was concerned the grant-in-aid for the year had been approved. Where was it, and why had it not been sent to us? We were desperately paying out small sums ourselves just to keep things ticking over. In yet another letter to Wadley John wrote: 'As you know, I had to ask Miss Welle to come down from Molo to help us out. The school started yesterday and we need money desperately. I have not been able to find suitable lodgings for Miss Welle and as a result she is having to pay £1 a day at a hotel … May I please have your suggestions as to what I should do to get this money as quickly as possible? Also, would it be in order for me to spend some money from my own pocket for the time being with a view to being paid back when the grant is made available?'

In a letter dated 24th September, Wadley assured John that ' . . .

in principle the payment of a grant-in-aid during 1951 [had been approved]' and it was hoped to settle the necessary formalities in the near future. But the 'near future' stretched well into November with no grant. Eventually, on 6th December, Wadley wrote a formal letter stating 'approval has been given for the payment of a grant-in-aid to the Co-Racial Kindergarten School in respect of 1951. A voucher for Shs.10,870.00 will be forwarded to you as soon as possible.' The letter concluded 'I am directed to make it clear to you that this grant is a temporary one for 1951 and cannot be considered to establish a precedent for payment of a further grant in 1952 or subsequently . . .'. In other words, don't get too excited.

In a subsequent conversation with Verry Vasey, John learnt that a part of the hold-up in payment of the grant was caused by the problem of where it was to come from. It had finally been decided that to avoid any confrontation with and criticism from the European elected members, the money was to come from the Asian vote of the department. Why could Wadley not have explained this to us earlier? More importantly, why did it take so long to sort out? Who was hoping that delay would be the kiss of death?

These months of 1951 from July to November were the low points of the school's existence, when, but for the persistence of two or three people against the subtle and determined behind-the-scenes inactivity of its opponents, it could well have become extinct. Unable to identify the opposition, let alone get to grips with and adequately counteract it, we just tried to maintain our faith that, somehow, things would work out. Which, eventually, they did.

The gloom lifted a little towards the end of November when John received a letter from Margaret Porter, applying for the post of principal of the Co- Racial School. She had already been shown round the school by Mrs Kroll and knew what the job entailed. On the debit side was the fact that she was a nursing sister, not a trained teacher. But she had had some teaching experience in an African school in Nairobi of which her husband had been principal. If she was the answer to our prayers she appeared to be not quite what we had hoped for. But was it not better to keep the school going somehow, even if its educational standards might fall, and hope that given time, we could pull it up again? She was offered the job in time for the new term in January 1952.

In the event Margaret Porter proved her worth, working hard, keeping the school going and the children interested. She was, in fact, a life-line. Her two daughters, Jane and Catherine, were added to the school's roll. Another pupil was Michael John Seldon, whose father taught at the all-white Prince of Wales secondary school and was among those Europeans who deplored the segregation of education in the country.

Perhaps the standard of education did fall a little during the next two terms, but not disastrously so. However, Mrs Porter was a wife and mother who had made it clear she could not continue indefinitely taking full responsibility for the school. In due course she applied to be an assistant teacher under the new head mistress. Although the board of governors would have liked to continue employing her, the Education Department considered there was no need for a second teacher at that stage and had made no financial provision for one. A few years later, on the road from Arusha to Nairobi, she was tragically killed in a road accident when a zebra ran from the bush in front of the car in which she was travelling.

1952 dawned with the assurance that Sir Philip's target had indeed been achieved. We had set up a multiracial school and it had been viable for the required two years. Its infrastructure was undeniably shaky, its enrolment low and its future still insecure, but we had demonstrated the presence in Kenya of at least a few Europeans who wished their children to mix with those of other races, and this, we felt, would gladden Sir Philip's heart, surrounded as he was by recalcitrant settlers interested only in their own narrow concerns. In February of that year, when Princess Elizabeth and Prince Philip visited the colony, a little group from the Co-Racial School took part in a parade of school children at Government House. We were delighted when during the rehearsal Sir Philip Mitchell made a point of seeking them out and being photographed with them.

Moving away from Parklands

During all this involvement with the school, our 'other' life had of course continued. The photographic part of the business had expanded to such an extent that, as mentioned earlier, we took the plunge of moving into a very large shop in Hardinge Street (now Kimathi Street). As John was not slow to point out, this expansion could be traced to his spending our wedding present money on an expensive camera. And indeed this had been the beginning of his expertise in the field, which led eventually, in retirement, to the publication of his three books. We moved in August of 1952, leaving the Monks's in sole occupation of our old premises.

The friction between John and his father increased, though politeness was maintained superficially. One source of disquiet was that I was expected to work for half the salary I could command in any other chemist's in town, all in the interests of the family and, it was said, while the business was getting on to its feet. This did not seem unreasonable, as long as there would be a review in due course. Clearly I was suffering from latent feminism.

K's game plan had been to build a business empire in which each male member of his family would play their part. My game plan as I grew up was to qualify as a professional who would earn a rewarding and reliable salary, so enabling me to make life easier for my parents, compensating for the awful stresses of their lives during the 1930s depression when I was growing up and we sometimes had less than enough to eat. It would also provide me with 'the good life'. Marrying John had seemed not incompatible with that plan, and fortunately my parents' lives became somewhat easier during and after the war. It had been a joy when we first arrived in Kenya to be able to send them food parcels – though Ma, understandably, was not too happy about the increase in her grocery bills.

The flaw in K's plan was the failure of the younger sons to get themselves educated; but even without that, the fact was that our two game plans were not just incompatible, but irreconcilable. The absence of any real communication with John for some ten years exacerbated misunderstandings. The younger members of the family, who could comprehend only K's viewpoint, became unpleasant, so that we both began to feel the strain of such close proximity. I had no doubt that I was seen as an evil influence, the cause of John's divergence from what the family expected of him, but the truth was that he had changed long before I met him. Had he been a conventional Ismaili, I should not have married him.

Poor K! At considerable expense he had sent his eldest son off for a couple of years to get a professional training which would enable him to found the family fortunes; but that wretched war had intervened, and his promising son had become a rebel. With hindsight one can understand his frustrations.

With Shereen's arrival, our house was just too crowded. The business was expanding satisfactorily. We felt able to contemplate finding a house of our own, but were up against those restrictive clauses. That delightful man, Peter Colmore, a customer and a friend, took time out from keeping half Nairobi amused with his wicked impersonations, to toy with a little journalism and estate agency. He urged us at one point to bring a test case against 'restriction' as he believed it would not stand up in a court of law. We were dubious, couldn't afford to take the risk and certainly were too busy to get caught up in such action. Eventually Peter found us an attractive plot some five miles out of Nairobi, with a distant view of the Ngong Hills, Nairobi's only pleasing natural feature. But it was huge! We had wanted half an acre. This was five acres. Subdivide, said Peter, and sell off the end bit you can do without. This left us with the bit with the view, and an attractive pergola terminating in a small stone gazebo, a true 'folly'.

With characteristic courage, John went ahead, burdening himself with a large mortgage and insurance policy. The trauma of the next year was typical of all the horror stories one ever hears about builders and deadlines, but eventually we were able to move in. Each of the children had a room of his or her own. Our bedroom, with ensuite bathroom – no more outdoor sanitation – had a view from one window of the Ngong Hills and from the other of a spreading albizzia tree, from whose branches each morning a dawn chorus led by the most beautiful bronze sunbird summoned us back to consciousness. What bliss! And, being several hundred feet higher than the city, the air was clear, pure, and fresh. That vague depressive feeling which had come to pervade the old house, shaded as it was by gloomy grevillea trees, not to mention family disapproval, all disappeared.

Golden wattle with its mimosa-like flowers grew for close on a hundred yards along the far boundary and they, together with the moonflowers and the white frangipani we planted, filled the air with fragrance for much of the year. We acquired a pink frangipani too but its flowers though pretty had hardly any scent. Another sweet-scented shrub was the curiously named 'yesterday, today and tomorrow' (a brunfelsia), which was simultaneously covered with shades of mauve and white blossoms as their original deep purple faded with age. The garden was a child's dream, with several terraced levels, and though the 'folly' was not a tree house, it featured in many of their games. When we moved in in late 1952 Shereen was just over a year old and content to be left with her ayah for the mornings, though my heart was wrenched each time we left her, to drop off the boys at school in Parklands, en route to town.

The bottom boundary of our garden coincided with a narrow

tongue of the Kiambu African Reserve, an anomalous division, it seemed to us, consisting as it did of a small valley whose opposite bank, a mere stone's throw away, was again part of Nairobi municipality. The original surveyors had perhaps not envisaged such expansion of the town. Just over our hedge were two *dukas*, or small African-owned shops. These were a boon to our servants, though not to us. They stocked little for our needs, but seemed to provide a plentiful supply of illegal *pombe*, the local liquor, to which our *shamba*-men (gardeners) were all too devoted.

A state of emergency

Two months before we moved, the government declared a state of emergency. This is better known as the Mau Mau rebellion, and was allegedly led by Jomo Kenyatta, a man we had met on one occasion after his return to Kenya in 1946 but with whom we had failed to communicate on any level, a not unusual occurrence at cocktail parties. Kenyatta had spent some 14 years out of Kenya, mostly in England, where he had married an English woman, and partly in Russia. This latter fact, together with his political activities in Kenya in the 1920s, notably as General Secretary of the Kikuyu Central Association which agitated for the African's right to the agricultural land which they saw as having been appropriated by white settlers, made him a natural suspect in the eyes of the administration, with the possible exception of Sir Philip Mitchell.

Kenya's security forces, and thus, members of LegCo, had for some time been aware of unrest in the Kikuyu reserves, and the belief had grown among the white settlers that Philip Mitchell was altogether too soft, too ready to believe that things could be sorted out amicably. In the words of Dick Frost, Mitchell 'was an idealist with a strong practical sense, a realist with an ideal of inter-racial harmony on which to base his policy'. Hardline settlers were utterly opposed to him. At one stage Mitchell said '. . . the country could have made great progress in politics and relations between communities had there been anyone among the European Elected Members able and willing to lead and to see further than narrow self interest, largely governed by fear.'

Philip Mitchell's departure as governor in July of 1952 threw into doubt the fulfilment of his promise of five acres of Government House grounds as the site of an expanded school. His successor was Sir Evelyn Baring, whose immediate task was to assess the threat of unrest by the Kikuyu and allied tribes, as a result of which the state of emergency was declared in October of that year.

Once more, our contact with the authorities was through our friend Verry Vasey, and in early January of 1953 John was asked to meet Sir Evelyn's private secretary in Government House grounds to measure out the site. He considered that 3.5 acres would be adequate. No firm lines were drawn other than on a plan by the Commissioner of Lands, and part of the land was cleared and levelled in rudimentary fashion. In practice, when the move was accomplished, if the children's games could be enhanced by overflowing into the governor's portion of the grounds, overflow they did. A fallen tree trunk and neighbouring bushes outside the school boundary served as a pirate ship, haunted castle, a glade in Sherwood Forest, or just plain 'house' to generations of Hospital Hill children.

An earlier meeting of the board of governors of the school had recorded among other things that buildings in Government House grounds, formerly occupied by Kenya Girls High School (a Europeans only school for which magnificent new premises had recently been built elsewhere), would be available for us. Necessary repairs and alterations would be undertaken by the Public Works Department, and subject to the consent of the Colonial Office, £8,000 would be made available to cover capital costs, plus £1,000 per annum for four years to meet recurrent costs. The Kenya government would be expected to meet any shortfall beyond this. It was emphasised that all this was 'confidential', no doubt to avoid any embarrassment to Sir Philip from those so strongly opposed to any form of multiracial education. He had been in London in March where his personal intervention had been responsible for gaining such welcome recognition of what we were trying to achieve.

From early 1953 things began to accelerate. Though Sir Philip had moved on, his legacy to us was sufficiently secure to preserve the school from extinction, and Evelyn Baring, who had until recently been British High Commissioner to South Africa, saw clearly that the old racial attitudes were doomed. His vision was to give Kenya a sound economic basis, developing industries and moving towards independence, and that would only be success-fully achieved if the population was educated. But first, the Mau Mau rebellion must be put down and all his energies were there directed.

Sir Evelyn himself took no direct interest in the school but his aide-de- camps were of a different calibre from their predecessors and we soon met some of them socially. One of them, Anthony Grigg, had loved Kenya from childhood, when his father Sir Edward Grigg (later Lord Altrincham) had been governor of the colony. Tony occasionally strolled down the back drive of Govern-ment House to visit the school and one day his eye was caught by a large 'clock' mounted on a tree in the parking area which recorded progress in raising funds for a school piano. Next day the school received a hand-delivered letter from Government House enclosing a handsome cheque from Tony. The letter read, in part, '. . . to the best school in Kenya'.

Under a new education ordinance John was approved by the department 'to undertake the management of a school'. The new emergency regulations made this a mandatory requirement for all schools as some, especially if up-country, were suspected of shielding Mau Mau terrorists. A school board meeting in March had enlarged its size so that it now included an African business-man, Dedan Githegi, and Ted Clarke's wife, Doris, who had been active in the United Kenya Club.

The Public Works Department, having estimated the cost of alterations and additions to the wooden buildings at a rather horrifying £4,000, soon began work – though not soon or fast enough for us. Scott Dickson, with his specialised knowledge, was charged with the job of recruiting a new headmistress from Britain. A selection board there, on the basis of her training, career and character, had recommended Mrs Eileen Walke for the post, at a salary of £690 p.a., with a cost of living allowance at 30%. She was asked to begin her duties in September.

Long before this of course, the question had arisen of what to call the school. 'Co-Racial', as well as being clumsy, would no longer be suitable as we were determined to expand and take African children as soon as we could. Philip Mitchell's advice had been to settle for something wholly innocuous, 'otherwise you will bring the wrath of all your enemies down upon your heads. Why don't you name it after the road leading to it, Hospital Hill?' And thus it became. The road was so-called as it lead, uphill, to the Government European Hospital. (In fact, the school was on Arboretum Road, at that time a rough unmade road which lead off Hospital Hill Road to the arboretum).

On 30th July Kenya's leading daily, the *East African Standard*, carried a headline, 'Inter-racial school to be opened in Nairobi.' It went on to relate that the Secretary of State, Oliver Lyttelton had approved a Colonial, Development and Welfare grant of £6,000 for the purpose, and the Kenya government's contribution to the recurrent cost would rise from £600 in 1954 to £2,000 in 1956. LegCo on the previous day had voted an additional provision of £4,135 to reimburse the Civil Contingency fund, and agreed to further expenditure of £1,365 during 1953 to purchase permanent equipment and for the payment of staff.

The newspaper went on to explain that the school, 'the outcome of a privately sponsored school which has been in existence in the Westlands area for about three years, will accept European, Asian and African pupils'. Mr Wadley, director of education had said 'the school . . . was perhaps the first concrete attempt on the part of the authorities to break down the colour bar . . . Asians . . . had spent a lot of money out of their own pockets, but the stage had now been reached where they could not carry on without some assistance . . . We think it is a very valuable experiment . . . but it has no chance of success unless the job is done properly . . . In other words, to make the facilities equal in every way to those of, say, a European school,' he added.

This public revelation of the school's existence created a certain furore and the acting chief secretary, Richard Turnbull, gave an assurance to LegCo that there would be no extension of inter-racial education without reference to the legislature. Accusations of breach of privilege were bandied about, but it was clear that although all white unofficial members of LegCo were against the scheme, we had won the first round.

Into new premises on Hospital Hill Road

At last – on Monday 14th September 1953, Hospital Hill School opened its doors in pristine new premises in Government House grounds under the headship of Mrs Eileen Walke, newly arrived in the colony, but with many years teaching experience in India, and with total commitment to making a success of multiracial education.

Clearly, with adequate funding now assured, a start must be made with recruiting African children. Our aim was parity among the three races, but we were too pragmatic to expect it in the beginning, and the board, optimistically, set the initial target at 16

Asians, eight Europeans and four Africans. But what did we have? We had precisely 11 Asian pupils (we personally had always rated our children as 'Asian'), the leftovers from the old Co-Racial School. What had happened to the 'Co-' bit? They had been the Europeans, long departed to schools of their own race because of the prolonged delays and uncertainties of the past year. So we must start again.

By the term's end we had our first African, John Mwathi, the eldest son of Dr Samson Mwathi who had replaced Dedan Githegi as a school governor. Three more children of this eminent family were to follow their eldest sibling through Hospital Hill. Sadly, one of the Mwathi boys was to die tragically in a traffic accident some years later, while still a student.

January 1954 opened with the school roll showing five additional African names. Another Mwathi, Peter; Marsden Madoka, who went on to become aide-de-camp to Kenya's first President, Jomo Kenyatta, and eventually managing director of Kenya's largest breweries, a distinguished sports administrator, and now a member of parliament and Kenya's Foreign Minister; Simeon Saidi, who went into banking; Wanjiru Waruhiu, who became one of Kenya's first women doctors and whose grand-father Chief Waruhiu was murdered by fellow Kikuyu for his resistance to Mau Mau; John (later Udi) Gecaga, who went on to business success and at one time was married to President Kenyatta's daughter Jeni; and his sister Mary (later Noni) who was actually not in the main, government-funded school, but in a small nursery class.

This was another hugely encouraging development. The Raineys had arrived in Nairobi some months earlier where Reg was a scientist with the Desert Locust Survey. True to form, the Education Department did not tell them of the existence of Hospital Hill, and they had enrolled their children, Paul and Janet, in a European school. When she heard on the grapevine of Hospital Hill, Margaret Rainey, a trained nursery teacher, rushed up to see Mrs Walke, keen to help in any way she could. As a result, a small nursery class was established in an adjoining building, using some of the old furniture, other materials being covered by fees. Margaret worked without remuneration. Her small son Roderick was a pupil, as was our daughter Shereen, Mary Gecaga, Agnes Mwathi, and Sheila Thakore, all of whom would graduate into the main school, a total of five 4–5 year-olds.

But tragedy was to strike. Janet Rainey fell ill one day – and was dead the next. It was polio. The shock waves ran through the school, and one dear soul went out of her way to tell me of seeing Janet the previous afternoon with her arm round my daughter's shoulders. But all pupils were at great risk. It was an epidemic and the city's chief medical officer closed the school for three weeks, as he had already done to the European school Janet had attended. It seemed so terrible that a family like the Raineys, such talented, gentle, modest people, dedicated to doing their bit in contributing something to the community in which they lived, should suffer so cruelly. They left Kenya shortly afterwards.

Our own doctor, dear Guy Johnson, recommended complete immobility, and prescribed daily doses of a barbiturate which would make it easier to keep our active three in bed. No shouting or singing either. Overtired muscles are most readily affected by the polio virus, so bed-rest seemed a sensible precaution. In bed they stayed for three weeks, during which period Nairobi's toyshops were denuded of all paints and painting books, reading books, puzzles, and anything else which might divert and entertain them. Though I was there almost all the time I'm sure in my absence they all hopped out of bed and had a little run around.

It seems highly unlikely that the children were in fact infected, but keeping them in bed gave us some obscure comfort. We were, we felt, **doing** something, were not entirely impotent in the face of this threat to their lives. Even today there is no cure for polio, which is transmitted by personal contact, but immunisation did become available soon after this sad incident.

A few days after Janet's death we were contacted by the city's chief medical officer and asked that parents of the five remaining children of the nursery class should bring them to a city council clinic next day for an 'injection'. This we all did, to the accompaniment of loud cries of anguish from our offspring. It was very mysterious, we were told only (even we, the pharmacists) that it had been brought in from South Africa at vast expense, and should help to provide protection against the virus. The injection was, we now conclude, gamma globulins, now widely used as a prophylactic against hepatitis and other viruses, but then only recently identified. Mysteriously, perhaps by the grace of God (but why, some might say, did He take Janet?) no one else in the whole school developed the dread disease, and slowly and sadly things began to return to normal, but with no nursery class.

The attitudes of the white Christian community

A warm and friendly personality, Eileen Walke was an unassertive but quite remarkable woman. She was sustained and driven by her Christian faith, yet never attempted to impose its tenets and dogma on her pupils. To her, all children were children of God. She set an example, and was dedicated to making them aware of the wonders of the world, realising their full potential and growing up as tolerant and even loving human beings. In her difficult role in a racist society she had expected to find support among the Christian community. This was not to be.

Citing the Roman Empire, Machievelli had noted that to be ruthlessly effective, empire builders needed to divorce the pursuit and handling of power from their morality as Christians. This alienation of the pragmatic from the spiritual self was certainly evident in Kenya. Consequently, sorely in need of support and friendship as Mrs Walke was, these were not forthcoming from the Anglican community.

For some time she lived in the YWCA hostel, roughly half way between the school and the Anglican Cathedral of All Saints. Here, the Very Reverend Evan Hopkins was the provost, and here she worshipped each Sunday, introducing herself to him quite early on. The general Anglican policy of the time was to refuse the sacrament to divorcees. As Eileen Walke came into this category, albeit as 'the innocent party', Evan Hopkins felt he could not allow her to take communion and this deprivation, with the consequent lack of community support, she felt deeply.

Marjorie Cooke, (now Partridge), also recently arrived in Nairobi, became Mrs Walke's friend and confidante and says that 'the one positive effect of [Eileen's] attendance at All Saints Cathedral was her meeting with its African curate, the Rev. Alan Madoka. When he sought to enrol his son Marsden as a pupil of Hospital Hill, she was overjoyed. After her disappointment at the reception she received from the "white church" there, this show of support renewed her faith . . . and her belief in multi-racialism . . . It gave her renewed strength' to dedicate herself to her belief in the truly Christian ideal of all people regardless of faith, creed or colour learning to live together in peace and harmony.

Eventually, under the apparently more liberal and laid-back Raymond Harries, the atmosphere at the cathedral – and probably in Anglican communities world-wide – did begin to change. But by then Mrs Walke had left Kenya.

In his excellent book on the Kenya of the day, *Race Against Time*, Richard Frost refers to Evan Hopkins in glowing terms, coupling his name with that of David Steel, pastor of the Presbyterian church in Nairobi, who went on to become Moderator of the Church of Scotland, and who in our view was a much more admirable character. The Reverend David Steel did not go so far as to send his own children to Hospital Hill (perhaps because the length of their stay in the country was uncertain) but, to publicise it among his parishioners, he did invite one of Hospital Hill's governors, the Reverend Scott Dickson to write about the school in the monthly St. Andrew's journal.

Pointing out in his article that, to succeed, the school must attract European children, he ended by saying, 'Just think with what pride your child will one day say, "I was one of the first pupils in the first of these schools."' David Steel's sister, Elizabeth Steel, in Kenya on a sabbatical, taught at Hospital Hill for a term and, he tells us, frequently recalled the joy of that experience.

Evan Hopkins would undoubtedly have had difficulties with his Anglican flock if, in befriending Eileen Walke, he was seen to be promoting the idea of multiracial education, yet he did indirectly make a contribution to it. He is credited by Frost with the revolutionary step of appointing as his curate in 1953, the first African to hold such a post in the 'white' Christian church in Kenya. This was, of course, the Reverend Alan Madoka, who was from Taita, and it was his son, Marsden, who became one of the first African pupils at Hospital Hill. Marsden's enrolment, as a sign of African approval of the school, brought great pleasure to Mrs Walke.

Much later, in retirement, she related to a friend in England her memory of a visit to the school by the Bishop of Mombasa. No doubt the publicity which the school attracted during the emergency had brought it to his notice. This devout woman had derived solace from the support his visit seemed to indicate.

Mrs Walke's teaching methods

Our children are of one mind, that their days at Hospital Hill were the happiest of their school lives. One potential problem frequently put forward by those who considered inter-racial education impracticable was that of religious instruction. The board agreed that 'the normal undenominational (sic) religious instruction should be given at the school', and no real problems were ever encountered. At a later period the leaders of one religious sect to which some of the pupils belonged requested a period for religious instruction, and a time was set aside for this. Other denominations were invited to send a teacher to instruct their followers too. This arrangement continued for about a year, but finally expired from apathy.

The day began with a reading or song, sometimes a poem, not specifically Christian or Muslim, Judaic or Hindu, but with some sort of spiritual or uplifting content. It sounds off-putting but was skilfully crafted by Mrs Walke and ensured a happy start to the day. Lessons duly followed, but sometimes a serious maths lesson, scheduled for 30 minutes, could well end up two hours later in a discussion of literature, painting or music. Mrs Walke tended to wander through the syllabus and beyond as the fancy took her, opening up the world and its wonders to her fascinated pupils. Is this not education? It was certainly fun.

At break, with their snacks and cartons of milk, the children erupted into Government House grounds where the semi-wild playground served as the perfect site for imaginative games. One type of eucalyptus tree had opposite branching, and these young branches made wonderful broadswords, shields being constructed from cardboard. On city screens of the time films such as *Ivanhoe*, *Zoro*, and *The Prisoner of Zenda* stimulated much imaginative play. In those early days the children had little in the way of sports equipment but the grassy tree-lined surroundings provided a fine arena for rounders and cricket. My son now tells me that they also played 'Kiss Chase', boys against girls. Just as well that the Education Department representative took so little interest in the school!

Not only resourceful, Eileen Walke was a talented draughts-woman, producing on the blackboard elaborate drawings

illustrating the stories of history and scripture she described so
eloquently to her pupils. Albert Schweitzer, Grace Darling, Moses
and his burning bush, the pharaohs and the pyramids, legends
from Indian folklore, were among the topics which held the
children spellbound. But a sound grounding in maths and English
was also imparted. 'My grammar's brilliant,' says one ex-pupil. 'I
can identify an adverb at 50 paces.'

Exploiting another talent, Mrs Walke started Scottish country
dancing, a skill our sons found a great asset when later they went
away to school at Gordonstoun. Papier mache puppets of
characters such as Scrooge were made by the children, resulting
in acting opportunities they all loved. The geography of Kenya
was imparted by following the railway line from Mombasa to
Uganda, making it of great significance to these youngsters who
had almost all travelled on it as it wound its way through Kenya's
fantastically varied habitats, from the ocean through coastal scrub
and desert, on to the Tsavo National Park, past Nairobi Park and
along the side of the Great Rift Valley, with its freshwater and
alkaline lakes, and the corresponding wildlife.

Attracting European families

This was all very well, but without a significant European intake
the school was a sham. Something must be done to counteract the
campaign of sabotage by Europeans in the Education Department
who blatantly omitted to tell newcomers about the country's only
multiracial school. The Raineys were not the only example of
which we learnt.

The governors addressed themselves to the art of seduction.
How to attract those waverers who seemed sympathetic, yet
continued to patronise all-white schools? Many European women,
even with husbands in well paid jobs, worked. There were no

work-permit regulations to protect local labour, cheap domestic help was readily available and though some women were happy to fill their days with golf and bridge, others were not. The snag for those who wished to work full-time was that standard 1 to 3 pupils in government schools did not attend afternoon classes, which meant their mothers could not conveniently work a full day. Hospital Hill resolved to fill the gap .

Doris Clarke worked out the menus for a week, an experienced African cook was engaged, trestle tables, folding chairs and kitchen equipment was bought, and each day those Hospital Hill pupils who wished, had a good hot meal at minimal cost. But could the youngest endure a full day's schooling? Of course not, even though the afternoons were devoted to undemanding things like puppetmaking, art, games, and the like. Out I went and ordered from Ahamed Brothers some 15 folding canvas beds (the firm kindly donated four of them) and after lunch the bigger boys set these up for the mandatory half hour's rest. Poor Mrs Walke must have been glad of that short respite too.

In fact, it had become too much for her alone and at the beginning of 1954 the Education Department agreed that an extra teacher should be taken on. Local candidates were interviewed. They were not always ideal and rarely full time, but one, Hilary Fitzgerald Finch, became a tower of strength to Mrs Walke. In 1956 Doreen Mackenzie was recruited from Britain and her youth and energy were great assets, both academically and in improving the standards of physical education and sport. Another overseas recruit in 1957 discovered that the social pressures operating against a European teacher in a multiracial school in Kenya were more than she could cope with, and she departed.

For me personally there was one positive aspect to this incident. The teacher concerned had signed a contract with the board of governors committing her to three (or maybe it was four) years of service, and on the strength of this they had paid her fare from Britain. She was now liable to refund this outlay and while we all felt sorry for the young woman we could not afford to write off her debt. The board authorised me to take the requisite documents to its lawyers so that they could pursue the matter. Here I met for the first time the rising young lawyer Mirabeau da Gama Rose. I was stunned by his good looks and charm. His abilities were no less impressive and the board soon received its refund. Mirabeau is more than tangential to the story of Hospital Hill as he later married one of its finest and most loyal teachers, Anne Innes. John gave Anne away when they married at St Xavier's Church in Nairobi and we count them among our dearest friends.

Early in the first term of 1954 Mrs Walke rang us in great excitement. She had been visited that morning by Mrs Dora Reiss and her three young children. John Reiss had recently been posted to Kenya by the Colonial Office as chief information officer, so he for one had circumvented the Education Department when enquiring about schools. Initially he had been enthusiastic, his wife less so, but when she and the children visited the school they liked what they saw, to the extent of feeling brave enough to rise above European public opinion. Martin, Judy and Jackie Reiss became the first white children at Hospital Hill. Reassured by this example, several more followed, though building up the European contingent took time. (Dora Reiss has since confided that the school 'made a difference to our attitude to the so called "race relations" and to John and me has been an advantage in our diplomatic life'.)

An additional incentive was the fact that Hospital Hill would charge European children only £5 per term, in line with other European schools. Soundings were taken. Would any of the Asian parents, for so long the school's loyal supporters, generous beyond measure when any extras were needed, would they feel badly treated if asked to continue paying the usual higher fee of £8? Not on your life. Some offered more. And what of the Africans? Samson Mwathi and John interviewed the parents and enquired about their financial situation, swallowed hard, and set their fees at £2 per term, and in one case only 15 shillings, to be reviewed in due course. An unexpected interest by the Motor Mart Trust, one of whose trustees had heard of Hospital Hill from Louis Leakey, resulted in their generously awarding top-up bursaries for the African students in those early years, so that the school was not out of pocket.

Eliud Mathu, an unofficial (nominated) African member of LegCo wrote asking that boarding facilities be provided at the school to enable those Africans living outside Nairobi to avail themselves of this wonderful opportunity for a better education. Please, Mr Mathu, where would we get the money for that? Running a day school was difficult enough, God knew. But let's keep it in mind for the future.

Next problem. Mrs Walke could not live indefinitely at the YWCA which was adequate as a temporary measure but not exactly luxurious or even homely. Adjacent to the long wooden four-roomed building which housed the school was another similar but much smaller one. Could that not be adapted as a house for our headmistress? Well no, actually, because a Mr Jarvis ran a Bible school there every Sunday afternoon. Surely so Christian a gentleman would agree to find some other suitable accommodation for the two hours a week which was all he needed, to enable a needy woman to live more comfortably? Well no, actually. Because Mr Jarvis, an ear, nose and throat surgeon, did not believe multiracial education should be encouraged. So he was staying put. We lobbied, we struggled, and eventually, after a year we got him out, but Mr Jarvis was strong in the Lord and hung on to the bitter end.

In marked contrast, when once the hut became available and had been repaired and painted, the parents, mainly Asians – Ismailis, Muslims and Hindus (Vimla Prem Krishen, wife of the then Indian High Comissioner to East Africa, whose son Pradip was a pupil, lent a whole suite of bedroom furniture) – turned up laden with spare pieces of furniture, discarded yet still serviceable curtains, a gas cooker and anything else they thought would contribute to Mrs Walke's comfort. One of the original five, Remu Verjee, who with his brother ran the country's most successful fish business, Kenya Fish, lent one of his lorries to transport the heavy items, as he was to do in subsequent times of need. The board, of course, provided Mrs Walke with anything else she may have needed. Fortunately, this building was well within the 3.5 acres of land granted to the board by the government at a peppercorn rent.

Consolidation

The years of 1954 to 1957 were ones of consolidation. Scott Dickson, who had been so steadfast in the most difficult days, resigned as a governor and left Kenya because of ill-health. Derek Erskine, Miss Welle's saviour in the saga of her work permit in 1950, joined the board, and enrolled his five-year old son Charles as a pupil, thus raising the school's social status in the eyes of those susceptible to such things. (He was an old Etonian.) This unconventional man and his wife Elizabeth became great supporters of the school and what it stood for, as they were of the United Kenya Club. Derek was eventually knighted in 1964. .

In 1957 Ronald Dain arrived in Kenya to replace Scott Dickson as general secretary to the Christian Council of Kenya. He was an educationalist and a recently ordained minister, who had been inspired to leave his teaching career for this post. Almost immediately he was co-opted to fill the vacancy left by Scott Dickson's departure and the experience he brought was a considerable asset over the years to come.

Another name closely associated with Hospital Hill is that of Gloria Hagberg, a white American whose daughter Paula was already enrolled as a pupil. Gordon Hagberg arrived in East Africa in 1956 as public affairs officer in charge of the United States Information Services (USIS). Early in the century his parents, Americans of Swedish origin, had been missionaries in Lamu. They had taken a dhow to Zanzibar to be married there by the American Consul. Both Gordon and his wife were totally devoid of racial prejudice. Gloria, a physics graduate, was appointed in 1957 as a teacher 'on temporary terms' when one British teacher had fled in the face of European settler pressure. (In the event, Gloria retired, aged 65, as deputy head under the school's first Kenyan headmaster, Julius Njoroge, in 1978.)

Some time in 1954 I was asked if I would take the minutes of the board of governors meetings. As honorary secretary to the board I continued to do this and much of the correspondence which gradually accrued so that Mrs Walke's burden was reduced as much as possible. My experience with the Education Department while chairman of the Aga Khan education board proved extremely useful. I continued in this role until David King's arrival, but when Mrs Angus became headmistress she dealt directly with the department. (I made notes in longhand at meetings, and dictated the minutes next morning to John's secretary.) The early formation of a Parent Teachers' Association (PTA) ensured generally good relations between the two components and helped channel efforts in fundraising. I was elected its first chairman but later incumbents were much more energetic in the role.

As the Mau Mau rebellion was brought under control, it became clear that Evelyn Baring was working towards independence for Kenya and that this would not be long delayed. Africanisation of the civil service, of local government, of the teaching profession, would follow inexorably – and colonial rule had prepared few Africans qualified and capable of filling such roles.

By 1958 Gordon Hagberg was in Washington at the office of the African-American Institute as vice president of operations, and became closely involved with airlifts of African students to colleges in the USA. The Americans did a fantastic job in

99

providing intensive education to hundreds of young Africans (thereby planting in them a preference for American rather than British mores and equipment, an error compounded some years later by Margaret Thatcher's imposition of higher fees for overseas students at British universities). The Hagbergs made an immensely significant contribution to independent Kenya. In his book *Freedom and After*, Tom Mboya put on record the considerable assistance given by the Aga Khan to the airlift programme, by providing £5,000 to help students with the £105 pocket money each had to have before they were cleared to fly. He gave similar amounts on several subsequent occasions.

Until Hospital Hill appeared on the scene there had never before, in Kenya, been a grant-aided primary school operating under a board of governors. Matters needing urgent attention had had to be postponed until the board's position had been regularised, which happened with the gazetting of a government notice establishing The Hospital Hill (Governors) Order 1954. It was formally agreed that 'the school syllabus should be as that laid down in the official "Syllabus for European Primary Schools", and that the pupils should be permitted to take the Kenya European Preliminary Examination, on the assumption that they would be allowed to proceed to their own racial secondary schools if they passed at a sufficiently high level.' The notice also required the appointment of four trustees. One of these was Carey Francis, principal of the Alliance High School, who expressed a high opinion of Hospital Hill School.

It was about this time that the Royal Technical College was founded in Nairobi, with the understanding that it would, as in fact happened, eventually develop into a university. So we had the ludicrous situation where children could learn with other races from age five to twelve, then had to be banished to a single-race school for six years, after which they could return to study with those of other races. Sex had something to do with this. Mix them when the hormones began to flow? Good heavens, that might well result in more couples like the Karmalis. Definitely not to be tolerated.

Ibrahim Nathoo, one of the contributors to the purchase of the original hut, was by now Minister of Works with two children at the school, and it was felt that he would be the most suitable chairman of the board, to which position he was unanimously elected. All governors were to serve for three years, with an option for re-election should they so wish.

Attracting international attention

The emergency, declared in late 1952, had rocketed Kenya into world headlines. Journalists flooded the country, and the political and social aspects of life there were reported and analysed in depth and detail in most leading newspapers in the West. It was a healthy phenomenon, letting in the first small puffs of the wind of change. After a while fresh angles on the emergency became elusive, and journalists cast around for other newsworthy topics.

Quite suddenly, Hospital Hill and Mrs Walke found themselves the centre of interest. Eventually, the situation got out of hand, and the number of visitors became so large that lessons scarcely got a look in. There was a danger that the more photogenic of the pupils might have their heads turned.

Early in 1955 two British journalists, Mr Edward Ward and Miss Marjorie Banks (in private life Lord and Lady Bangor) came to Kenya to work on a programme on the emergency for the BBC. Broadcast in Britain in April, it described, according to *The East African Standard*, 'the war against the Mau Mau, and strongly advocated setting up multiracial schools to solve the problem of the younger Africans' future'. The Wards had spent many hours in previous weeks at Hospital Hill, recording the children at work and at play, and in their televison programme they 'stressed the hope they felt for Kenya's future in the young children attending the one multi- racial school that has been established, with white, brown, and black races represented'.

The Ward's programme was shown on primetime TV by the BBC and we and other parents received excited letters from several friends and family who quite unexpectedly recognised our young on the screen. None of us saw it ourselves, but we did receive still photos from the papers, which greatly gratified our children. Permission of the board was presumably sought for the BBC to film at the school. We have no recollection of meeting the Wards and as Ibrahim Nathoo was chairman at the time, they must have dealt with him. There is no written record.

In addition, the issue of 2nd July of the British magazine *Illustrated* carried a pictorial feature by them on the school, 'Kenya's School of Hope'. Their article began, 'The three races in Kenya must learn to live together if peace is ever to return to that land. That is the deeper problem behind the Mau Mau troubles,' and went on to indicate their cautious optimism after visiting Hospital Hill – 'black, brown or white ... here they are just children'.

Kenyan journalists suddenly became aware that in their midst there existed an experiment in multiracial education which was attracting tremendous interest overseas, and they had all but neglected it. *Tazama*, the Swahili paper produced by the East African Standard group, published a full double-page spread with eight large photographs plainly showing children of all three races working and playing together and looking remarkably happy about it.

The Sunday Post, at that time the only English Sunday paper in the country, was edited by Kathleen Robinson and owned by a man called Rathbone, who were both vehemently anti-multi-racialism. It was the first local paper to publish an in-depth article on the school, with photographs, on 3rd April 1955. Headed 'Verdict on Kenya's First Multiracial school – The Pupils are

"Colour blind"', it was by-lined 'Sunday Post Reporter'.

The article began by noting 'the crisp criticism of a noted Nairobi European (you all know him) . . . "A Welsh accent and a mass of complexes about table manners and race relations – that's about all you'd get from a multiracial education."' We personally certainly did **not** know the man referred to, but his views were typical of most Europeans in the colony. Over a two-page spread the reporter strove to remain objective. 'The surprising thing about Hospital Hill School,' she says, 'is that it is so "undifferent" . . . it is quite true to say that nowhere did I find the slightest trace of "race-consciousness" among the children. They played and worked in complete and happy companionship, utterly blind to the differences in skin pigmentation.'

She complained that where the Kenya government had lacked the courage to make up its mind, the Colonial Office (referred to as 'outsiders') had gone ahead, heedless of European antagonism, and drew the conclusion that inter-racial secondary schools would surely follow. (This article undoubtedly helped mobilise the opposition which indeed eventually scuppered efforts to establish such a school.) Great play was made of Mrs Walke's reluctance to answer questions, 'almost as though she had received instructions not to commit herself on points of policy or allow a visitor to fasten on to facts which might give scope for criticism', comparing this to 'one of those tours behind the Iron Curtain where everything is almost too wonderful to be true'.

But, significantly, the article concluded with the following paragraph: 'It is all so perfectly natural. In fact, so natural that after a couple of hours at the school I no longer noticed that a black boy was sitting with a white girl, or that fuzzy hair is so different from golden tresses. It became just an ordinary school.' What a wonderful admission!

There was nothing sinister about Mrs Walke's reluctance to discuss school policies. There was nothing to hide. As headmistress she implemented decisions made by the board, which

instructed her to refuse to be drawn into discussions of their aims
and methods, but to refer enquirers to them. She was already fully
stretched by her teaching schedule, much of the school's administration, and overt animosity from Europeans. The board sought to
protect her wherever possible. (The newspaper did not contact the
board of governors for further information.)

The Sunday Post reporter was also very suspicious of pupil
selection, accusing the board of admitting only children of
outstanding intelligence who showed promise of unusual scholastic ability, chosen to 'blazon the advantages of multiracial
education . . . a good propaganda move'.

The board's actual target was to run a school of high standard,
with parity between the races, and for this reason, while European
enrolment lagged behind, many Asian applicants had to be turned
down. Paradoxically, we had, in that limited sense, and for a short
and limited period, to behave in a racist manner. In the first year
admission had been confined to children coming from homes
where some English was spoken but that requirement was soon
dropped when experience proved it to be unnecessary.

Patently, children of parents who cared sufficiently about racial
harmony to want to send them to a pioneer multiracial school of
a high academic standard, were intelligent, and may have had
'unusual scholastic ability', but no attempts were made by the
board to assess this and no selection was made on these criteria or
any other, with the one exception mentioned above. The time was
to come when the demand for places by all races became so great,
that the waiting list was in its hundreds. Probably the only thing
Hospital Hill had in common with Eton was that many parents
put down the name of their child for admission at birth.

Interest in the school was not confined to East Africa and
Great Britain. On 16th July 1956, under the byline of Leonard
Ingalls, an American correspondent of international repute, a
factual report was published in the *New York Times*, recording that
the school now had 38 pupils with three teachers. 'Ten of the

JGK with my parents and younger sister June in Rhyl, 1937.

In 1948 the then Aga Khan visited East Africa with his 15-year-old younger son, Prince Sadrudin, pictured here with 'K',
(John's father, Karmali Mohamed), and John.

A Karmali family group taken with Prince Sadrudin.
Back row: Jimmy Ahamed, JGK, the prince, Badrudin Kanji,
John's brother Haji, 'K'. Second row: Dadima, Ma,
(John's blind mother), and his sisters Nurbanu and Sherin,
various grandchildren, including Jan.

Nelda Welle (later Mrs Kroll), encouraging the campfire to prosper,
at an Open Day for parents when the pupils of the
Co-Racial school wore fancy dress.

In June 1952, a member of the royal family was due to visit Kenya, and schools were invited to Government House the previous week for a rehearsal. Sir Philip Mitchell, the Governor of Kenya, made a point of seeking out and being photographed with the pupils of the Co-Racial School. (Mrs Margaret Porter was headmistress at the time). These are: Back row: Aly Ibrahim Nathoo, Zelobia Verjee, Aditi Pant, Katherine Porter, Amin Gwaderi, Yusuf Keshavjee, Jane Porter. Front row: Jan Karmali, Tazim Kassam Kanji, an English girl (name forgotten), Sir Philip Mitchell, Peter Karmali, Michael John Seldon, Nassir Badrudin Kanji.

Sir Philip Mitchell chatting with John & JGK at a function in early 1952.

In 1953, as chairman of the Aga Khan Provincial Education Board, talking with the then Governor of Kenya, Sir Evelyn Baring, after he had opened the newly built Aga Khan Primary School in Nairobi.

With the school building in the background, Peter Karmali, Judy Reiss, Naseem Nathoo and Marsden Madoka on their way home after school.

Fun with the puppets they had made! Patrick Moore, Zulie Ahamedali, Judy Reiss, Martin Reiss, Marsden Madoka and Jan Karmali.

Mrs Walke adjusting Naseem's tie, watched by Marsden, Mrs Deacon and Martin.

Twin desks are shared by children of different races at Nairobi's Hospital Hill School. Pictured in this class: three Asians, Zulie Ahamedali, Yusuf Keshjavjee and Zelobia Verjee; two Europeans, Adrienne Moore and Martin Reiss; and one African, John Mwathi.

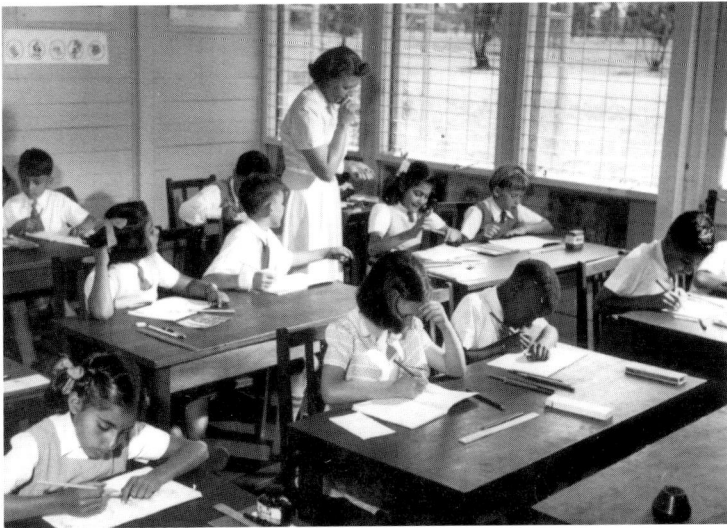

Mrs Eileen Walke in her classroom at Hospital Hill.

In May 1955 we went on leave to Britain. I was amazed at how many friends and family came to wish us well and see us off from the old Eastleigh airport. They include Hannah Vasey right of John; on the left, his three sisters, Sherin, Nurbanu and Malek; his cousin and brother-in-law Shamsu Ahamed front row right, and Mahan Singh front row left.

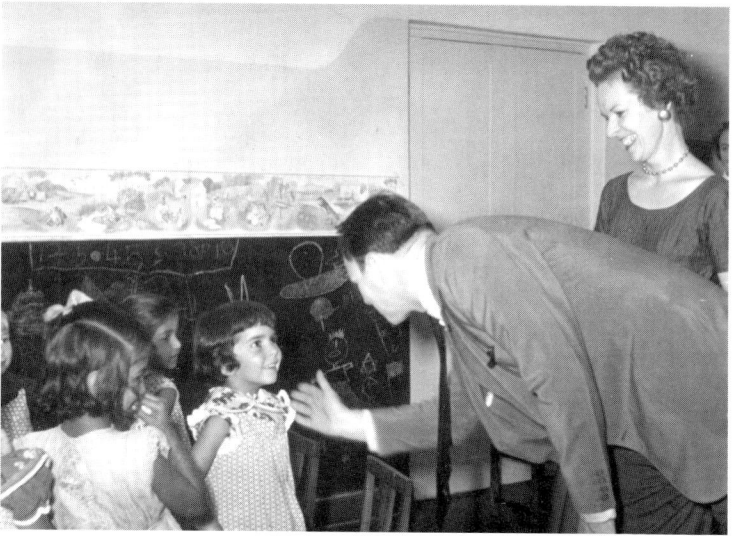

Prince Aly Khan came to visit Kenya in the mid-fifties.
Showing him round the new Aga Khan Nursery School,
I couldn't resist introducing him to Shereen.

Prince Aly with the Provincial Education Board members:
Left to right, Zubeida Thobani, Hadi Kothari, JGK, Prince Aly,
Mr Ibrahim Kara, Madatali Alibhai Sharif, Amirali Karmali
(no relation), Rahematali Abdulla, Shamsu Nimji.

JGK about to show Rita Hayworth, Princess Aly Khan, round the Aga Khan Girls School.

Shri Apa Pant, Indian High Commissioner to East Africa, with Rita Hayworth and Prince Aly. Ibrahim Nathoo stands behind Rita Hayworth.

A 21 Club dinner at Chez Dave in honour of one of the Tata brothers from India, right to left: Hassan Rattansi, JGK, Achroo Kapila, the young Nairobi lawyer who at the time, was part of the team defending Jomo Kenyatta at his trial in Kapenguria.

April 1957, at the Aga Khan Primary School, the farewell party when I had resigned and was about to take my sons to school in Britain.

On the Kenya coast about 1960, Shereen happy to be reunited with Peter and Jan when they came home from Gordonstoun for the summer.

Derek Erskine and John (Udi) Gecaga out with the Limuru Hunt, the photo which so enraged some settlers!

August 1961, on holiday at Vipingo, Back row – Jan, Amin Gwaderi, Marsden, John (Udi); Front row – Shereen, Peter and Mary (Noni).

Break time at Hospital Hill in Government House grounds.

Mrs Mollie Angus, with members of her staff at Hospital Hill.
Fourth from right: Doreen MacKenzie. (Others included Mrs Borstlap,
Mrs Hawksworth and Miss Rao).

Mrs Angus with her top class in 1962, the last term before the move
to Parklands. They include Shahina Jaffer, Sallie Cooper,
Aneesa Kassam, Mary Gecaga, Sophie (Sopiato) Likimani,
Florence Amenya, Sheila Thakore, Masood Thobani, Sheema Kanji,
the Kassim-Lakha twins and Salma Tejpar.

In January 1962, Tom Mboya married Pamela Odede and before the large official reception at the City Hall, Charles Njonjo gave a celebratory lunch at his home: John, Pamela, Tom, JGK, Tom's brother Alphonce Okuko and Gulie Rattansi.

Sir Derek Erskine and JGK re-fuelling at the Mboya reception.

Because we had had such a quiet wedding, we decided to throw a big party to celebrate our Silver Anniversary in December 1968. Our old friend Charles Njonjo congratulating us.

Group of friends at the party, from left, Jenny Nathoo de Angelis, Sherbanu Nathoo, Hassan Nathoo, Vittorio de Angelis, JGK, Madatali and Zubeida Thobani, John, my special friend Hannah (Lady Vasey).

At a garden party in City Park for the visit of the Queen Mother. John, who was then an alderman of Nairobi City Council, JGK and Sir Ernest (Verry) Vasey, then Kenya's Minister of Finance.

In May 1968, four newly built classrooms in the Hospital Hill premises in Parklands, were opened by the then American Ambassador, Glenn Ferguson, seen on the left, then Kyale Mwendwa, Charles Njonjo, Joel Wanyoike (City Council Education officer) and John.

children are Negroes (sic), twenty are Asians and eight are white." Ingalls pointed out that while segregated schools were still official policy, 'those responsible for the multiracial school . . . feel deeply that in time integration will be recognized as a practical means of achieving race harmony among Kenya's mixed population'.

In Britain's *News Chronicle* George Vine spoke of children lining the roads to greet Princess Margaret, then on a visit to Kenya. Would she notice the little group standing by the gates of Kenya's Government House, he wondered. The only exceptional thing about this particular group of 45 children, he continued, is that they will be mixed up. 'Mixed up, I mean, in the most uncrazy way – physically jumbled together, flaxen-haired Europeans standing beside woolly headed Africans and sloe-eyed Indians . . . probably the most important thing that has happened here in the last four troublous years. It is the Colony's first and only inter-racial school.'

Mrs Walke's four year contract would come to an end in the summer of 1957 and everyone hoped she would be prepared to renew it. Sadly, she had news of the serious illness of her sister who lived in Britain, and broke it to the board early in the year that she would not be returning. In the event, she left a few weeks earlier than expected as her sister's condition rapidly deteriorated, bringing to an end Hospital Hill's important formative years. She left behind an invaluable legacy, a foundation of harmony and happiness that none of those who knew them would ever forget. The fact that academic standards were not yet of the very highest would soon be put right.

Eileen Walke was totally 'colour blind' and consequently so were her pupils. They emerged from the school to face their new worlds, full of confidence and with lively minds, well informed on all kinds of topics, in not all of which examiners may have been particularly interested. Many went on to do well in whatever walk of life they chose, readily catching up on their academic careers and often noted for their attractive and well adjusted personalities.

Two of those who emerged to face new worlds were our sons, Jan and Peter. We had gradually and reluctantly come to accept the fact that establishing a multiracial secondary school was unlikely to happen in time to accommodate them when their happy days at Hospital Hill came to an end. We had to face a decision, to consign them to the government's Indian secondary school or send them overseas. English public schools had to be considered even though we had always deplored the social divisions they created. We wanted academic achievement for our sons, but even more important was a school's attitude towards race. The choice narrowed to two, Bedales and Gordonstoun. With hindsight the former might have been a better choice as it would have been so much more accessible to visiting friends. But we were told that while it did much for girls, boys did less well there. Correspondence with Henry Brereton, and a subsequent visit to Gordonstoun, convinced us that our young ones would suffer less there from racial prejudice than in other schools, and though Gordonstoun's academic record was not brilliant we were persuaded that under its new headmaster Robert Chew this would improve.

In April 1957 I took the boys to Britain to kit them out, and they began in the summer term, initially, as they were just 12 and 10, in Gordonstoun's prep schools, Jan in Aberlour House and Peter at Wester Elchies. I was distressed that they were not together as we had been promised but there was nothing to be done When for half term I took Shereen and my mother up to stay in Elgin, the boys seemed happy enough, but as those few days ended their homesickness was painfully apparent.

We spent a happy summer holiday together, mostly at my sister's farm in North Wales, and when they returned to school Shereen and I flew home to Kenya. My family provided loving support to Jan and Peter. It was my sister June and her husband Emlyn Williams who provided the stable background of a happy home for them during their school holidays; and my mother's younger sister, my aunt Ethel, who mothered and fussed over them on the occasions when they were in transit in London between Scotland and Kenya or North Wales, and sent them the home-baked cakes and goodies I was too far away to provide. Nevertheless there were times when they were acutely homesick.

In Kenya too this was an unhappy time. Home alone in the afternoons, I could not stem the tears. I missed my sons so much that I was forced to wonder if we had done the right thing. But we had made our decision in the light of the prevailing circumstances and I could only hope that it had been, ultimately, in their best interests. Thereafter, until their schooldays were over, they spent only seven and a half weeks a year at home, though I did see them too in the years when I was able to visit Britain.

The changing political situation

To place the development of the first multiracial school in its proper historical perspective one must recall very briefly the political developments which followed the declaration of the state of emergency in 1952. This in effect meant that the British policy of delegating responsibility to colonial officials and settlers had failed. The Colonial Office had to work out a new policy, and successive colonial secretaries began to initiate changes, starting with the Lyttelton Plan published in 1954. Under this Africans were given a limited franchise, and one African and two Asians became ministers.

1957 brought the Lennox-Boyd Constitution. Now there were to be eight African elected members in LegCo instead of six nominated ones as previously. Twelve specially elected members, four of each race, were to be elected by LegCo sitting as an electoral college. The MacLeod Constitution of 1960 provided for the majority of ministers to be Africans. All three constitutions

107

were multiracial and as such totally unacceptable to the Africans. Negotiations continued, and led to complete independence for Kenya by December 1963.

The Mau Mau rebellion and consequent state of emergency had given all sections of Kenya's population food for thought. It was clear that the governor, Sir Evelyn Baring, was set on implementing British government policy, and while utterly against this, the European settlers nevertheless knew there was a certain inevitability about it. They fought their corner with as much implacability as they could muster. One move was to set up a separate European Education Authority and a special committee of the European Advisory Council on European Education had been established. They were hopeful of support from the Christian Council of Kenya of which Ronald Dain, a governor of Hospital Hill, was education secretary.

But in July 1955 he had sent to the ministers of education and finance, and to the director of education, a lengthy report setting out the CCK's approach to the problems of inter-racial education, some general principles which it felt should govern future experiments in that field, and concluding with the view that the next step should be provision of an inter-racial boys boarding school. This, the CCK suggested, should commence at preparatory or primary level, developing in time to a full secondary stage. Such a school would need to be supported by government grant-in-aid.

It was, then, hardly surprising that when Ronald attended one of the meetings of the European group on 25th July 1957, he was less than sympathetic to their aspirations. I quote from that meeting's minutes:

> Mr DAIN explained that although he wished to give every assistance to the committee in examining the financial implications of the establishment of an Education Authority, he was unable, on professional grounds and in the light of 25 years experience in educational

administration, to give his support to the proposal that such an Authority should be set up. The Christian Council of Kenya was also opposed to the Authority but on entirely different grounds, with which, however, he also agreed.

Mr E.R.BLOCK considered that without the official support of the CCK it would be more difficult to persuade Government of the desirability of establishing the EEC, and that the two bodies should meet to discuss their opposing points of view with the hope of resolving them.

The CCK, through Ronald Dain, issued a lengthy document setting out its views, urging the setting up of independent boards of governors for all senior institutions such as colleges and secondary schools, comparable to practice in UK and the Commonwealth, and applying to all racial groups. 'It [the CCK] has considered that any open attempt to secure special treatment for the most favoured community cannot but arouse suspicion, fear, and bitterness among those who are less favoured,' it stated, and later '[it] cannot, on grounds of Christian charity or justice, support a policy of racial discrimination or differentiation'.

All of this was unexceptionable, so it was somewhat surprising to learn from Colonial office documents of the time that the CCK, whose spokesman was Ronald Dain, while urging a Christian basis for any multiracial secondary school, used language like 'accepting the infidel as a fellow traveller'. Else-where, in a conversation Dain had on 18th November 1958 with the Minister of Education, Labour and Lands on the same topic, it became clear that he thought Hospital Hill Primary School had begun as a Christian project and feared a weakening of this force as 'it was liable to drift into largely Asian hands'. One can all too readily take things for granted, but I find it amazing that Dain could have been unaware of the religious tolerance which had characterised the foundation, and indeed the whole life, of the school. Without the initiative of Ismaili Muslims, and a Hindu family, as well as headteachers of the Christian persuasion, there would have been no multiracial school in Kenya until independence. In spite of their record of some mixed schools in India, even the Roman Catholics in Kenya had followed the settler line and there had been no initiative from the Christian community to establish one. One can now see that this intolerance of other faiths may well have been the main reason for Dain's eventual resignation from the board of governors.

However, we had always valued Ronald Dain's presence on Hospital Hill's board as, at the time, we did the initiative of the CCK. But the minister of education was firm in his reply to their representations. Any decision on an inter-racial secondary school would be made by the government as a whole, not by him personally. 'It is a subject on which there are wide differences of opinion,' he wrote, 'and on which many people hold very strong views.'

An editorial in one European-owned paper of the day, headed 'Mixed Schools', illustrated the dilemma of whites. It read, 'This is a difficult world, where principle is constantly being confounded by the brilliant exception. I am one of those who believe that the general introduction of mixed schools would be fatal for the future of Kenya, but the other day I met a little girl who told me her name was Zulekha Mahomet (sic). Her English was so perfect that I asked her where she had acquired it. The answer was, at the mixed school on the hill, where she was also taught Latin, French, Arithmetic, Algebra and Geometry. She was altogether charming. It is all very difficult.'

By a timely coincidence there appeared in the *Kenya Weekly News* of 26th July an article on the school written by one of its regular contributors, Sheila Dixon. This paper was aimed at the farming community, which in those days was made up almost entirely of European settlers, and was published in Nakuru, the 'capital' of the White Highlands. Perhaps the remarkably objective approach of the article's writer gave the more open-minded settler food for thought.

Sheila Dixon reported that as an experiment, the school must now be regarded as having succeeded. 'The atmosphere of friendliness,' she says, 'combined with discipline, is particularly noticeable. The children's manners are excellent but there is no feeling of restraint and none of them seemed to mind visitors looking over their shoulders at their work.' The secret of the spirit of harmony among these children from widely differing back-grounds, she presumed, 'was due to the fact that they began to share their life and lessons at the early age of six when they [were] almost completely unselfconscious, and would not normally make any differentiation between themselves and children of other nationality, race, or colour'.

What a wonderful vindication that was of everything we had always believed and hoped to prove. More perceptive – or perhaps better informed – than most other journalists who had visited the school, Dixon went on to discuss the big problem which these children would face when they were old enough to leave Hospital Hill, entering the anomalous system which provided only mono-racial secondary schools. She highlighted the difficulties, of which we were all too painfully aware, of suddenly providing an inter-racial secondary school at this stage.

But she concluded that Hospital Hill School's 'products will sail out into the world on an even keel, secure in the knowledge that mentally, culturally and socially they can take their places together on an equal footing in this land of Kenya which is the home of them all. If it be thought that this is a good and desirable thing, perhaps the Education Department will do something about increasing their numbers?'

It should be noted that these comments were made during Eileen Walke's time at Hospital Hill School.

The search for a new head-teacher

For more reasons than one the year of 1957 is a memorable one for us. Mrs Walke's understandable decision not to return to Hospital Hill precipitated a flurry of activity. Doreen Mackenzie, a young and dynamic teacher had been recruited from Britain the previous year. Though without experience as a headmistress Miss Mackenzie was perfectly capable of holding the fort until a new one was appointed. Gloria Hagberg was also on the staff, very supportive but reluctant to take any extra responsibility at that stage, having two children of school age as well as social commitments as wife of the director of the United States Information Service.

By now the Education Department was, mostly, on our side and they made efforts to find a replacement for Mrs Walke from Britain through the Overseas Appointments Board. But the school's finances were too limited to provide all that aspiring applicants hoped for, particularly a housing allowance. How fortunate we had been that Mrs Walke had been so amenable and understanding about our initial difficulties with accommodation, and how tolerant of the shortcomings of her little wooden house. One very committed applicant, a graduate, who had been shown over the whole place, found that his wife, arriving for the new term before him, realised too late that she could not tolerate so small a house.

For the first term of the new academic year Doreen, Gloria, and Mrs Gregory, whose husband had been posted to Kenya in the RAF and who was a gifted addition to the staff, soldiered on alone, very efficiently but at too great a personal price for this situation to continue in the long term.

Mr Stokes, in charge of European education in the department, suggested that the board should consider appointing Mrs Mollie Angus, recently retired as principal of Westlands Primary School, one of the foremost European government primary schools. On

6th January 1958 she took over. A number of parents with sons at the school had asked that a new principal should be male so that the boys should have not only a role model but someone to take their games. This was many years before the notion of 'equal opportunities' (which was explained to me by my grand-daughter when she took up rugby football!). In fact, Doreen Mackenzie was a splendid athlete and had livened up the school's sports considerably. But the idea had been planted, and it was explained to Mrs Angus that if a suitable man became available he could be appointed over her head. She fully accepted that this might happen and her first contract was therefore for only a year.

In due course it did happen, but the new headmaster proved anything but satisfactory, resigning after a short time, and Mollie Angus resumed as principal in May 1959. She could not have been more different from Mrs Walke. Eileen Walke's heart ruled her head, but though Mollie Angus had a heart it was undoubtedly subservient to her head. In a way, this was appealing. The school's ethos had been established, but when the first of its pupils, just before Mrs Walke's departure, sat for the Kenya Preliminary European exam, which would ensure their admission to a Kenyan secondary school, their performance, though creditable, had been less than outstanding. One of its first African pupils, Marsden Madoka, failed to gain admission to the prestigious Alliance High School in Kikuyu, which skimmed the cream from African candidates, and it was only through the personal intervention of ourselves with Mr Wadley that he was admitted to Shima-la-Tewa at the coast – and nearer his true home in the Taita Hills near Voi. (I still have two charming letters from Marsden written from Shimo-la-Tewa.)

By the time Marsden had begun at Hospital Hill, he was already nearly ten years old, so it had been an uphill struggle for this delightful boy. He was not very happy at Shimo-la-Tewa at first, among much older boys who looked on him as an oddity. But he went on to a brilliant and highly successful career. Such an example of triumph over adversity would have gladdened the heart of Eileen Walke had she lived to see it.

Mollie Angus was steeped in the ways, requirements, and methods of European education in Kenya, a favourite in the department, who knew her way around. Moreover, she was experienced in preparing students for the KPE examination and when John Gecaga entered in the following year, he passed into the Alliance High School with flying colours. But he too was initially unhappy in such an unfamiliar mono-racial ambience.

The board of governors was keeping a close eye on admissions and the racial ratios. In July 1955 the total roll had been 30, of whom 15 were Asian, 7 European, and 8 African. By the time Mrs Walke left, enrolment was 55, of whom 26 were Asian, 17 European, and 12 African. As always, some space was kept for subsequent recruitment of the last two races. At any time, the school could have been filled with Asian children. This would have been good for its finances but totally destructive of its multiracial *raison d'etre*.

The need for a multiracial secondary school

The time was to come when Hospital Hill's main problem would be lack of space but more immediately pressing was the need to provide a multiracial secondary school. Both Marsden and John Gecaga had suffered culture shock when they left to enter purely African secondary schools. They were boarders, and John especially found the diet of *posho* (maizemeal porridge, the African staple food) literally more than he could at first stomach.

His father, Bethuel (later Mareka – they abandoned their Christian for their Kikuyu names as independence loomed) Gecaga, had worked as a dresser at the King George VI Hospital, to which Hospital Hill Road led. It was the biggest hospital in

Kenya at that time, whose professional staff were all European. Gecaga worked for Bill Kirkcaldy Willis, medical missionary and orthopaedic surgeon, who had been among the founders of the United Kenya Club. Gecaga had considerable charm, was also a Christian and patently intelligent, and Willis took a great liking to him, perceiving that he had potential which poor levels of African education had failed to develop. He encouraged him to study further, personally tutored him in Latin and eventually ensured that Bethuel came to Britain to pursue his studies in law. (There must have been financial help but where it came from I do not know.)

Unfortunately for his wife Jemima, Bethuel had barely left when the state of emergency was declared. She was a probation officer and lived with their two children, John (Udi) and Mary (Noni) in rooms at Jeanes School in Lower Kabete, a considerable bus ride from her place of work in the city. As unrest, and consequently the activities of the security forces, increased, Jemima often found herself harassed when passengers were turned out of their buses, searched, and left stranded on the roadside for hours at a time. Hearing of this, the ever-generous Erskines insisted that Jemima and her children should stay with them in a flat over their stables. (The Erskines lived in a magnificent mansion at the end of Riverside Drive, complete with ballroom, the scene of many lively parties including the annual hunt ball.)

Consequently John and Mary became accustomed to a different diet – and a different way of life – from the traditional one. John also displayed an affinity for horses, which endeared him even more to Derek's heart. Seeing an opportunity to metaphorically thumb his nose at the entrenched segregationists, Derek arranged for a photo of John and himself, mounted and in full hunting gear, to appear in the local paper. Shock, horror! What was the old and secure world coming to when an African, other than a groom, took part in hunting? That maverick Erskine was at it again, encouraging Africans to rise above their station.

115

Amin Gwaderi was the first Indian pupil to leave the harmonious atmosphere of Hospital Hill and go on to a purely Asian school, and although his background was entirely Ismaili and he spoke an Indian language, even he was at first unhappy. We explored possibilities, but it was clear from the first that starting a secondary school from scratch was a very different proposition from a primary one. Laboratories, a library, expensive equipment, higher salaries, meant a large monetary endowment before it could be launched. Where could we find it? I extracted names of trusts interested in education from the British Council library, and, in innocence and hope, wrote off to some of them, speaking of the primary school's success and the resultant need. Not surprisingly, only dusty answers, if any, resulted.

New Kenyan friends

On a business trip to England in the early 1950s John had been taken to lunch by Sadrudin Walji Hirji – who had taken over our flat when we left London in 1946 – at an African students club near Marble Arch. Here he was introduced to Charles Njonjo, a Kikuyu in London to take his Bar finals and attend his dinners at one of the inns of court. It was a jovial lunch and they took to each other. In 1956 Charles, now qualified, returned to Kenya and was engaged to work in the attorney general's office, the first African to do so. He and Sadru Walji Hirji in fact travelled south by car across the Sahara. It may have appeared a foolhardy venture but it did show anyone who might be interested that not only Europeans were capable of rather daring feats. And it raised Charles's profile.

We met Charles again at a dinner party at the Rattansis'. He was essentially a shy man, finding himself immersed in more than one culture, but equally determined that if the country had a future, practitioners of these differing ways of life must learn to understand and respect each other. In Gulie and Hassan's lively and jocular company, the future weighed on us not at all.

Gulie had trained as a secretary but Hassan did not want her to work. While Hassan put in long hours in his grocery store in central Nairobi, she flitted about the city, calling in on her numerous friends, making new ones, passing on the gossip, flirting, entertaining and being entertained. Like most Ismaili women she was a superb cook and the Rattansis' parties were always well worth going to.

Charles's father was a Kikuyu chief, a man not only prominent in his own community but respected by liberal white politicians of the time. (Loretta Tremlett recalls attending a reception at his home in Kabete in 1956, given for a visiting British Labour MP, Eirene White). With the state of emergency now repealed, the Colonial Office was keen to be cooperative and employ (perhaps absorb would be a better word) educated and suitably qualified Kenyans, of whom there were pitifully few. Charles's immediate superior in the office of the attorney general, David Coward, was a congenial man with a pretty if conventional wife, and they took Charles under their wing socially, as well as David providing guidance in the workplace.

Gulie and Charles established a special rapport. Her gaiety and wit enlivened his slightly sombre nature (later to be transformed by a wonderfully happy marriage to Margaret Bryceson, and three delightful children). In the next few years, other 'returnees' were to be found at the Rattansi's parties. Kariuki Njeri and his highly intelligent African-American wife Ruth; Mungai Njeroge the American-trained doctor, brother of Jemima Gecaga; and very occasionally Julius Gikonyo Kiano with his wife Ernestine, also African-American.

Perhaps the most interesting and impressive Kenyan we met there was a man who had spent but one year overseas, on a scholarship at the British trades union establishment for further education, Ruskin College, Oxford. This was Tom Mboya.

117

In Western politics the phrase 'stabbed in the back' is a not unfamiliar metaphor. In untamed Africa, it, or its equivalent, can be all too real. Had Tom Mboya lived, been allowed to live, Kenya could have been a very different country today. His intelligence was outstanding, his determination inexorable, his shrewdness and astute insight equipped him to outwit his opponents where necessary, and his charm when he wished to use it, could be utterly irresistible. He was a true highflier and, perhaps most important of all, a man of integrity. Latterly some considered he had become arrogant. Our perception of him at that stage was of an understandable awareness of his own abilities and he was never less than friendly. Whether, had he lived, power would ultimately have corrupted him, one cannot know, but in those days, unlike some of the others, he seemed immune to perverted or cynical influences, including that of alcohol, as was Charles Njonjo.

At some stage John talked to Tom about Hospital Hill's difficulties, its desperate need for new premises for the present primary school and its prospects of extension to secondary level, canvassing his support. Soon after this conversation John and I were invited to Hassan Rattansi's for drinks. Tom was there, along with Mungai and Charles Njonjo, and a man we had not met before, Bruce MacKenzie. It was soon clear that Tom had engineered this little party so that Bruce could size us up. More than that, we got the message that if Bruce approved of us and our hopes for the school, so would Tom and Charles. And vice versa. We drove home, exchanging our impressions of Bruce, not knowing quite what to make either of him or his very apparent influence with our African friends.

Bruce MacKenzie was a white South African who had fought in their air force during the war. He was a rather coarse-featured man, with mutton-chop whiskers, who had married a white Kenyan girl and when the war was over, settled in up-country Kenya, managing her family farm. He became a European elected member of LegCo and about the time of the constitutional conferences in London, gained the confidence of Jomo Kenyatta. The agreement reached at the Lancaster House Conference of 1962 included the appointment, along with Mboya, Gichuru and several other black Kenyans, of Bruce MacKenzie as a minister of the Kenya government, in his case, that of agriculture.

Bruce's reaction to us and our plans for Hospital Hill School must have been favourable as from then on Tom always did all he could to promote the interests of the school. We were at first ambivalent about Bruce – as a person. Eventually we assessed him as a charismatic buccaneer, with a keen eye for an opportunity. As he was so close to Kenyatta, Tom had good political reasons for working with him.

We met Tom also in the home of Verry and Hannah Vasey. He was very close to Verry, who saw him as the outstanding African politician – and Verry knew them all. Among Verry's papers after his death was a small scrap of paper, an IOU from Tom acknowledging a loan of £300 which enabled him to buy his first car.

In Dick Frost's otherwise excellent account of pre-independence Kenya, *Race Against Time*, it is amazing to find only one reference in the index to Sir Ernest Vasey. Frost came from a quite different social background from Vasey. Clearly, they rarely if ever met, and Frost, unwittingly, gives most of the credit for establishing good relations between the educated young Africans and European politicians to Michael Blundell. (In his later book *Enigmatic Proconsul*, a biography of the then governor of Kenya Sir Philip Mitchell, Frost records Mitchell's opinion that 'Ernest Vasey, a most able and valuable Minister . . . will certainly be the first "premier" of Kenya.') While it is true that in time Blundell bowed to the inevitable and contributed considerably to harmonious race relations, as Sorobea N Bogonko points out in his *Kenya 1945–1963: a Study in African National Movements*, 'properly speaking [he] was a fence-sitter, and where he was not a fence-sitter he was for European supremacy'. Vasey had been a liberal for far longer, and the two men never became close.

Unlike Charles and Kariuki, both sons of wealthy chiefs and therefore brought up in relative comfort, Tom Mboya was born to a humble Luo worker on a sisal estate south east of Nairobi. Though not exceptionally brilliant in school he had done well enough to gain entry to the Roman Catholic Holy Ghost College from where he passed his African school certificate at a high enough grade to go on to Makerere University in Uganda, the only university in East Africa at that time. But his family was too poor to pay his fees, and he was instead recruited by the Kenya Medical Department, being sent for training at Jeanes School, Kabete. Here the large student population was made up of a number of tribes and age groups studying several different disciplines, and it was here that Tom's horizons broadened and he began to become politicised. Employed as a sanitary inspector by Nairobi City Council, it was not long before he became involved in trade union activities, and this became his power base.

Though he loved dancing and parties, he was essentially a much more serious character than some of the other prominent Kenyans who had been to university in Britain or America. Tom knew about the conditions of the African working classes – he was one of them – and he had learnt to rise above the negative aspects of tribalism. As a city council health department employee, with authority to inspect sanitary arrangements in any building, he, as recorded in a posthumous biography of him by David Goldsworthy (*Tom Mboya: the Man Kenya Wanted to Forget*), had personally encountered European arrogance and hostility when at least one white had rudely and unlawfully refused him access to her house. Consequently he was well acquainted with the country's racial inequalities and was a powerful ally when we at Hospital Hill needed support.

At one stage he invited us to lunch in parliament buildings to meet a visiting delegate from the Ford Foundation, and spoke persuasively of the need for help in expanding the primary and establishing a secondary extension of Hospital Hill School. Ford

Foundation had no remit to cover elementary education, but at one time we were very hopeful that they would help with the larger project. John had several meetings with Frank Sutton, the local Ford Foundation representative, but nothing came of it. The American consul general of the time, Dudley Withers (this was before Kenya was accorded the status requiring a full ambassador), though a friendly and tolerant man, felt he had to point out that, given the implacable opposition of the whites, overt American involvement in multiracial education would be a very hot potato indeed.

A lively social life

One of the things John and I had most missed when once we were settled in Kenya was the opportunity to go dancing, so we were delighted when several bright souls, including his cousin Jimmy Ahamed and an old friend Abdul Tejpar, started the 21 Club. Initially, monthly dinner dances were held in a private room in Torrs Hotel, but the atmosphere was less than congenial. The hotel's white clientele might protest vocally and probably physically if its air should be polluted by the breath of Asians and Africans – though it seemed to be alright if the black waiters breathed upon them when serving them food and drink.

But what was then the newest and tallest building in central Nairobi, Mansion House, had just been completed and its top floor restaurant, Chez Dave, was readily made available by its Jewish owner, Dave Singer. The club's aims, loosely stated, were to provide occasions where young people of all races who loved dancing, could eat, drink and socialise in a relaxed atmosphere, a kind of intermittent, non-intellectual, slightly frivolous, United Kenya Club. Its members were all Asian, mostly Ismailis, but the idea was that we should all invite guests of any race. We loved it.

121

I have only one less-than-happy memory of it, an unfortunate occasion when someone in our party had invited an eminent colonial servant and his wife, neither of whom could or wished to dance, and we had to endeavour to keep the evening going with what was inevitably pretty frigid conversation.

One irony of Nairobi's social set-up was that Jews were considered to be barely one step up from Asians and Africans, not to be compared with the putatively pure-blooded European. They too were barred from membership of exclusive clubs like Muthaiga, yet the country's best hotels were owned by Jews, most conspicuously the Block family. Abraham Block was a remarkable man. His family, like so many others, had fled Russia and its pogroms at the turn of the century and settled in South Africa.

In 1903 the British, still with a mighty empire and now influenced by the Hungarian-born leader of modern Zionism, Theodor Hertzl, was still actively seeking a national home for the Jews. At that time Kenya's northern boundary was just beyond Naivasha and north of that the territory was part of Uganda. An area near Eldoret was suggested as a possible Jewish home, and 12 members of South African immigrant families were selected to visit and judge its suitability. Ten of them rejected the site and returned south almost immediately, but Abraham Block felt he had little to lose and elected to remain. To earn a living, he began dealing in cattle.

Doing well, he bought a small farm at Limuru. Doing even better, in the 1930s he bought from the Tate family the Stanley Hotel at the very centre of Nairobi. By then, his two sons, Jack and Tubby, were grown men and able to take over much of the running of the business, quickly expanding to acquire the Norfolk Hotel, the centre of settler folklore, especially connected with the colourful personality of the pioneering Lord Delamere, who had contributed much to the development of the country's agriculture, and had lost much of his own wealth in the process. Jack and Tubby's sister, Ruth, had married an accountant, Sol Rabb, who contributed greatly to the financial stability of the outfit. (They were to become two of our closest friends.)

Our lives as pharmacists

There were also interesting events to do with the pharmaceutical side of our lives. The first occurred about 1950/51, before we moved out of the original Portal Street premises, above which were the surgeries of the five doctors I mentioned earlier.

One of these doctors, William Boyle, came into the shop and asked John to step out on to the pavement for a moment. He handed John a prescription for morphia, in the name of a prominent titled British socialite, telling him that she had just arrived in Kenya, and was registered with the British Home Office as a morphine addict. Dr Boyle was therefore authorised to prescribe a regular monthly supply of the drug for her, of which this prescription was the first. She had become addicted some years previously after the drug's use in relieving post-operative pain and was on it, at a controlled dose, for life. Many people were similarly recognised by the Home Office. John was asked to treat the matter with the utmost confidence, which he did, apart from telling me the circumstances as I would be dispensing the morphine.

We came to know the patient well. She was a woman of exceptional beauty and charm, grey-haired by the time we knew her. It was not difficult to imagine how she had swept London society by storm in the 1920s and 1930s, and made more than one successful marriage. Very friendly, bright-eyed and amusing, she clearly had as great a rapport with animals as with humans and would habitually arrive in the shop with a pet hyrax draped round her neck. When she invited us to lunch at her home in Karen we were impressed by her brilliant hand-painted murals on the dining room walls.

123

Another 'pharmaceutical' anecdote is about Sir Evelyn Baring, who succeeded Sir Philip Mitchell as governor of Kenya in 1952, and lost no time in introducing a state of emergency. By then we had moved our shop and dispensary out of our tiny place in Portal Street and into much larger premises at the bottom of Hardinge (now Kimathi) Street. By coincidence, at almost the same time, the Boyle and Johnson practice moved into a modern building almost opposite us.

Sir Evelyn Baring had served overseas in several tropical countries, notably Egypt and India, as well as his previous posting to South Africa. It appeared that while in India he had picked up an intestinal parasite (probably an amoeba), which had affected his liver. As a result, he needed daily medication, as prescribed after investigation by doctors at the School of Tropical Medicine in London. Long before we opened up in Nairobi, Government House had run accounts at the then leading pharmacies in the town, Howse & McGeorge, and Wardles. Embarrassingly, these firms found themselves unable to dispense the governor's prescription, so it looked as if supplies would have to come from London. But first, the aide-de-camp decided to try us. Could we dispense Sir Evelyn's pills? We certainly could.

Like many professions, pharmacy has changed beyond recognition since the war. The skills we diligently acquired at university, preparing pills, suppositories, various emulsions and unguents, are now undertaken wholesale by the machines of manufacturing companies. But at the Square we had had to polish these skills and in setting up our pharmacy in Nairobi had equipped ourselves with whatever we thought we might need. The pill machine was a case in point.

The preparation of pills was quite a skilled process, their active ingredients being meticulously weighed out on our most sensitive balance. (Dosages could be as low as a small fraction of a grain.) Placed in a mortar, an excipient, usually lactose, was gradually mixed in. With the aid of liquid glucose, a substance even stickier and gooier than honey, a homogeneous mass was achieved, in which the dispenser must be satisfied that the active drug was evenly distributed. This was then rolled into a long thin pipe, just long enough to stretch across the pill machine's hundred grooves, all this with the aid of a little pure talc to counteract stickiness. The grooved plate of the 'squashed rolling pin' element of the pill machine was placed on top, pressed hard down – and you were left with 100 little brown pieces, which you proceeded with your fingers to squeeze into something approaching roundness. Pharmacy folklore had it that the best way to make your pill mass cohere and not split was to use a little spit. Fortunately I never had to resort to this technique.

The next step was to perfect the 'rounding'. This was a most relaxing interlude, when one could safely gaze into space and contemplate the universe, while soothingly revolving a small wooden disc over the little brown pieces until they became approximately spherical. A final, so to speak, gilding of the lily, could be achieved by shaking them up with several thin leaves of silver which coated them, though I do not recall doing this for Sir Evelyn. I made his pills regularly until he left Kenya, and this episode certainly meant that in future we received a fair share of Government House business.

Eventually pills went out of fashion and factory-made tablets took over the market. What happened to those who needed a specifically prepared remedy? I have no idea, but would guess that specialised pharmacies like John Bell & Croyden in London's Wigmore Street will still prepare them.

Hollywood comes to Kenya

Guy Johnson, who had become our family doctor and encouraged Shereen into the world, was as interested in

125

photography as he was in music. Whether it was as a result of these twin interests or through contacts of his cousins' Phil and Peter Johnson who had the city's primary accountancy firm, he became involved in films. He was appointed medical consultant to the film company which made *The African Queen*, much of which was shot on the Nile in the area of Murchison Falls in Uganda, and starred Katherine Hepburn and Humphrey Bogart. Guy spent a lot of time on location. We were given the task of providing all the medical supplies and equipment the film unit needed, and a year or so later he and we performed a similar function for the film units making *Mogambo*. By this time we were ensconced in the bigger shop in Kimathi Street and frequent visitors when they were in Nairobi, particularly to the photographic department, were its stars, Clark Gable, Grace Kelly, and Ava Gardner. At the time she was in a stormy marriage to Frank Sinatra, who followed her to Kenya. John recalls helping him to get to grips with a twin-lens reflex camera – and I remember how much shorter Sinatra was in real life than he appeared on film. He looked an insignificant little guy in a baseball cap and at first I did not recognise him. But the blue eyes were brilliant and he was completely relaxed and friendly.

The school grows under Mollie Angus

Although past government retirement age, Mollie Angus, when she took over as headmistress of Hospital Hill School in January 1958, hit the road running. Managing a primary school was child's play, and she clearly relished the prospect of some reorganisation. Her excellent relationship with the Education Department was much to the school's advantage and she possessed the knack of getting on well with her staff. The atmosphere was very different from Mrs Walke's day, brisker, more businesslike. This was not undesirable so perhaps it was because of my affection for the previous incumbent that I never felt quite the same rapport with Mrs Angus. She had previously worked only in the European system. So far as we were aware, she had never exhibited a passionate devotion to the idea of multiracialism, but was patently untroubled to find herself running an inter-racial school. It was a mutually satisfactory arrangement.

Partly because of all the publicity and partly because of the school's reputation under Mrs Angus, enrolment took off in the next year or so. In three years it almost doubled, from 68 in 1958 to 124 in 1961. By 1963 it was up to 200. With small classes (the rooms were too small to accommodate many more than the board's ideal of 20 to 25 pupils), we were a full single stream primary school. The place was too small. What could be done? All available space in the elongated wooden building was in use, and all that remained for conversion to a classroom was what had been Mrs Walke's sitting room.

The quest for a bigger site

Before things got out of hand the governors discussed possibilities for expansion. One was to persuade the governor to give us permanent tenure of the piece of his grounds occupied by the school, expand the building and create proper playing fields. Evelyn Baring was in fact very sympathetic to this, but felt he must leave the decision to his successor, Sir Patrick Renison, whose arrival was imminent. Renison would possibly have agreed to five acres, but the loss of ten acres was, understandably, not acceptable.

Then we must look for a site, preferably of government land, which would cost us little or nothing. Our chairman, the Honorable Ibrahim Nathoo was not only a member of LegCo but by now minister of public works, surely well placed to bring pressure to bear? Siting was important, for many of the African pupils travelled to school by bus, and complicated changes on to yet other buses in the city centre were undesirable for such small children.

May 1960 brought the offer from government of five acres at Mbgathi near their King George VI Hospital (the very same after which the school was indirectly named). At first this seemed a satisfactory site. Fortunately, active in the PTA at that time were several experienced and committed civil servants, S F (Bill) Bailey and Oliver Knowles in particular, and an eminent and articulate architect, Richard Hughes, who eventually became a governor of the school. They did some research – and discovered that not only had the adjoining plot been allocated by government for a new mental hospital, but that the offered site was situated down-wind from the existing Infectious Diseases Hospital. Anything more calculated to discourage new parents from choosing the school could hardly be imagined. Knowles wrote an eloquent letter to the governors, setting out these and other disadvantages. It may have been paranoid to think the offer of this plot was deliberate, but there could be no doubt that some of those civil servants dealing with the school's future were less than committed to it, and might well have hoped for its demise.

The next offer was of a site in the Kilileshwa suburb of Nairobi. Though accessible, it was far from ideal. Derek Erskine summed up its unsuitability in a letter to me in November 1960. 'Our acceptance of the Kilileshwa Site would for all time peg the Hospital Hill School as a Single Stream Primary, comparing very unfavourably with the European Kenton College 400 yards away, and four times the size. (I note that the Kilileshwa site is only twice as large as the St. Nicholas School for 16 backward European children, almost next door).' Derek was strongly against 'any poky little sites in Nairobi', and, mind fertile as ever, went on to suggest the ideal, a 20 acre site within Nairobi City

128

boundaries in a decent part of Nairobi, adding that he knew of no other such area than his own Riverside property! This was investigated by the commissioner of lands among others (Derek was influential, a member of LegCo who was also a school governor) but access would be beyond the already made-up road, and miles from any existing bus-stop. For these reasons it was a non-starter.

The third possibility was Maryland, a plot previously occupied by a riding school, further from the city than Kililehswa but nearer areas where some Africans lived. Things were getting desperate so Maryland had its attractions. But before a firm decision could be taken, Bill Bailey discovered that the plot had already been allocated to the police.

Arguments flowed back and forth. John was concerned that parents at a recent PTA meeting seemed convinced that when an African government came to power – which was by now readily foreseeable – it would be sympathetic to Hospital Hill and allocate 10 acres of Government House grounds to it. Nothing, he had told them, was further from the truth. When all schools became multiracial, in theory if not always in fact, there would be no reason to give our school special consideration. (Sadly prophetic words.) And as Joan Holland, the then representative of the department on the board, rationally pointed out, there would not be enough Europeans and Asians in the country to maintain the policy of parity between the races.

The related problem was that even if we found a suitable site, where should we find the money to build on it? Gordon Hagberg, back in Washington with the African American Institute, had sympathetically cast around for possible help. Through him John and I had met several visiting Americans who might be helpful, most importantly Professor Francis X Sutton who was director of the Ford Foundation. Tom Mboya, always sympathetic to our desire to open up good education to the non-European population, invited the three of us to lunch with him in Parliament Building, the main thrust of his and our plea being that the foundation might put aside in this instance its commitment to funding only higher education. Frank Sutton, a charming man who coped with the stresses of a heavy workload by playing the violin almost to concert level, was clearly swayed by the points we made – and Tom's passionate commitment to Hospital Hill would have carried a great deal of weight. These negotiations and others continued for months.

Ford Foundation eventually pulled out. Frank Sutton wrote to me that 'the difficulty, briefly, is that we cannot properly enter into politically controversial projects within countries or territories overseas'. He knew that I was also acting as secretary of a committee under the chairmanship of Humphrey Slade, a prominent white lawyer who had in the past held prejudiced views about race, but became the first Speaker when the newly independent Kenyan Parliament came into being. The committee planned to start up a multiracial secondary school for boys only (I hated this sexual discrimination, but my considered view was that half a loaf was better than none, which is why I had accepted Derek Erskine's invitation to become involved). Sutton added that, having clung a long time to the opinion that the multiracial secondary school project was free of such difficulties, the foundation had had to conclude that it most likely was not, and they could not, at present, be active in the support of multiracial school projects in Kenya.

An interesting sidelight emerges from a letter Gordon Hagberg wrote to me (on the African-American Institute's letterhead) in mid-1959. Gordon reiterated Ford Foundation's original favourable view of Hospital Hill School, adding that at one time they had allocated $50,000 for it. 'Then,' he said, 'we learnt that Capricorn was set to take over the project, at the request of Mr Coutts. This did not sit well with the Ford Foundation ... which had indicated a willingness to make considerable sterling sums available . . . I spoke to Very (sic) Vasey about this when he was here, and I believe some others did also; and he persuaded Mr Coutts to give up the Capricorn idea when he returned.' Gordon went on to speak of an 'ominous ring' about yet another floated suggestion involving some of the specially elected members of LegCo and a 'college for leaders' (this, presumably, was Humphrey Slade's project though I never heard it so described), finally concluding 'I think that if the new project is presented as a modification of the Hospital Hill plan, with three of the Hospital Hill Governors and yourself participating, the Ford people might make the $50,000 already approved available for the new scheme.'

The 'Mr Coutts' referred to was Wally (later Sir Walter) Coutts, chief secretary and onetime acting minister for education, who had been a good and helpful friend to us over Hospital Hill's difficulties, but presumably had sought to broaden the basis of its administration. 'Capricorn' was the fairly recently founded Capricorn Africa Society, which aimed to promote co-operation and harmony between all races in central and eastern Africa, and whose symbol was the zebra, which has some brown as well as black stripes on its basically white coat. Its founder was David Stirling and he primarily had Rhodesia in mind, though the society soon found some support in Kenya. He was part of the large construction company Stirling Astaldi and undoubtedly aware of disadvantageous commercial effects should these restless countries be plunged into civil war. (Currently, the history of the Capricorn Africa Society is being written by Richard Hughes, who was an active and dedicated governor of Hospital Hill School, and who, as surprised as I was, kindly acquainted me with Ronald Dain's unsuspected prejudices).

For a time John was treasurer of the Kenya branch of Capricorn. In the brief contacts he had with the man, he was not impressed by David Stirling's sincerity. We should certainly have opposed any involvement of Hospital Hill with Capricorn had the suggestion materialised. This then, was the political contamination which caused Ford Foundation to draw back from funding Hospital Hill School.

In these few years before Kenya gained independence so much was going on both behind and in front of the scenes, so much lobbying, particularly by Europeans who could now see the writing on the wall and were manoeuvring to gain any possible advantage. The European Parents Group, of which Tubby Block was a leading and effective member, made a valiant attempt to set up a European Education Authority, to pre-empt development of integrated education, but failed. Even though we lost some of the battles, it was an exciting place to be at an exciting time, and we relished it.

The changing political scene

During the four years of the emergency, the collective psyche of Kenya had irrevocably altered and every community was aware of the inevitability and imminence of political change. Although it would still take time, anyone with any feel at all for politics knew that independence would be achieved and Kenya would, in the foreseeable future, have an African government. Over the next few years this provoked a rapid exodus of European settlers, some of whom had already sought sanctuary from a similar situation in India. They mostly went south, first to what was still Southern Rhodesia, some on to South Africa. The effects of this migration were numerous but what affected our situation was the fact that European primary schools suddenly had many empty places, to the extent that they were threatened with closure. There was even talk, behind closed doors, of taking some selected African and Asian pupils into European schools.

The situation at Hospital Hill School was radically different. Our waiting list was so long that we desperately needed more classrooms. We had nowhere to go, and no money to achieve expansion. This is best illustrated by quoting from John's speech as chairman of its board of governors at its annual prize-giving ceremony held in All Saints Cathedral Hall on 29th November 1961. Ironically, in view of the present state of Kenya, the guest of honour on that day was the then minister of education, Mr Daniel arap Moi, who was shortly to apply for places at Hospital Hill for his own children.

I quote:

> ... this is a special occasion ... [as] the school in its present form has come of age, so to speak. The KPE examinations this year were taken by a number of pupils who started their scholastic career in this school in Standard I. Standard VII next year [will] have a full complement of 20 students, also for the first time.

> ... what of the future? Some people believe that in view of the progressive integration taking place in Schools at primary level, Hospital Hill School has served its purpose and will become redundant in the near future. The Governors of this School are not of this opinion. We believe that it has still a very important part to play. It is still the only truly 'multi- racial' school as opposed to a merely 'non-racial' school. And by multi- racial I mean a school where it is the deliberate policy of the Governors to maintain a nearly equal ratio of all three races in the school. Furthermore, Hospital Hill is still the only school producing children of the right age and standard to feed non-racial secondary schools. It had also become apparent ... in recent weeks that if children in this country have to go to integrated schools, a number of parents prefer them to go to a school which already has some experience in multiracial education.

... pressure for admission is greater than ever ... [out of] nearly 180 applicants ... we could only admit 25. It makes us very sad to say 'no' to [those] who have had their children's names down for admission for so long, in some cases for over 4 years.

John went on to repeat the need for a bigger school and the board's difficulties in finding a suitable site. Most importantly, he reported that with the Education Department's blessing they had decided to start a second stream up to standard 3. The board was negotiating with Delamere Girls' School governors with a view to renting from them part of the premises adjacent to the existing buildings of Hospital Hill School. Provided suitable staff was available, the second stream would start in January (1962). This, he said, was but a temporary measure. The present school was bursting at its seams, the grounds were a dustbowl in dry weather and a very muddy swimming pool in the wet. The school had justified its existence and amply proved what it had set out to, that all races could be educated together, in harmony and friendship, without any lowering of academic standards. He praised the parents for their continued loyal support, knowing that the school's interests were very close to their hearts, and Mrs Angus for attaining excellent exam results in spite of the difficulties of accommodation.

The decision to introduce a second stream was underpinned by confidential information from the Education Department that, due to the European exodus, one of their primary schools was likely to become vacant, its remaining pupils being reallocated to one of the others. But no decisions could be taken until the European Education Advisory Council had met. Power still resided very firmly with the Europeans, who were fighting rearguard actions on every front. A 'Memorandum Addressed To Parents Of European Children in Kenya', marked 'Confidential, Not for Publication', was produced setting forth reasons why European and African girls should not be educated together. It was an unbalanced document, quoting selectively about African sexual habits from books by a Ugandan woman, Noni Jabavu, and Kenya's Jomo Kenyatta. Misleading though it was, one understood how frightening deep prejudices could be.

Hospital Hill fought back. Derek Erskine, soon to be knighted (an award made partly, which was richly ironic, because of his friendship and ability to get on with Africans, notably Jomo Kenyatta,) was to ask a parliamentary question. I drafted and John amended a memo on the school's need for new premises, making 11 points. We included the comment that the one school in Nairobi which was expanding, had a waiting list, and was considered suitable for educating the children of a number of ministers of the Kenya government and members of Legislative Council, was in totally inadequate premises, while enrolment in a number of other primary schools which had almost new and fully equipped premises, was rapidly diminishing. (There were in fact 800 vacancies in the Nairobi European schools, and Laurie Campbell, who was headmaster of the prestigious Alliance High School for African boys and a Hospital Hill parent, expected this figure to rise to 1,000 by the end of the year.) John ended with the assertion that unless the department made an immediate decision on the future of Hospital Hill School, the governors would be forced to consider the possibility of closing it down. This memo he circulated to various other ministers in addition to that for education.

Discussions on the possibility of taking over one of the city's other schools dragged on from early 1962. We were eventually told by the department that no decision could be made until admissions to European schools were finalised in mid-November 1963. Once again, every consideration was to be given to the European parents' viewpoint, and Hospital Hill could stew. David Gregg was the colonial servant with whom we dealt, and super-ficially smooth and sympathetic though he appeared, we had no doubt where his real sympathies lay. This was confirmed by subsequent events.

The Parklands European Primary School buildings

In December 1962 it was revealed to the local press that Hospital Hill School would be allowed to occupy Parklands School. On 14th December I wrote to the permanent secretary of the department (who was David Gregg) stating that we had learnt this fact from the newspapers, but that the board had had no official intimation of it. Reiterating the school's desperate situation concerning accommodation, I asked for confirmation, and a date when we could move in. Mr Gregg was above replying himself and his deputy Mr Amar wrote to me, saying, 'As you perhaps know, the parents of the Parklands European Primary School have been given the option of a terms notice before pupils are withdrawn . . . it appears that they will exercise this option and therefore it is unlikely that the buildings will be available before the second term 1963. I shall of course, let you know the exact date when you could move in. Meanwhile a suitable rent is being assessed.'

'Of course' and 'as you perhaps know'! The insolence of the Education Department and their absolute disregard for the interests of our pupils made me feel sick.

Parents had made it clear to the PTA that they were adamantly opposed to any suggestion of Hospital Hill pupils being redistributed among the half-empty European schools, which was apparently one idea which had been floated. When the newspapers reported that Parklands School was to be made available to Hospital Hill, Richard Hughes, the PTA chairman, wrote to *The East African Standard* responding to accusations by its headmaster, a Mr McCormack, that any of its pupils left behind there would become a small European nucleus in a school which, being multiracial, would have no interest in or obligation to it. This was arrant and mischievous nonsense, revealing either unfounded prejudice or complete ignorance of Hospital Hill or both. He, and the parents of his pupils, did not wish to be confused by facts.

At a board meeting on 11th February 1963 John reported that he, Mr Dain and Dr Mwathi, representing the governors, had met ten days earlier in the Education Department with the ministry's representatives, Messrs Mole, Frankish and Amar. From this meeting it emerged that Hospital Hill could take over the land and buildings previously occupied by Parklands Primary School without paying rent, but should undertake responsibility for repair and maintenance of the buildings and upkeep of the grounds – and also the necessary insurance. The assurance was later given that our tenancy 'should not be terminated by Government within less than 3 years of its first occupancy'. The meeting agreed that these terms, as laid down by government, must be accepted.

A rather unethical proposal

I then put on record some bizarre encounters I had had with both the ministry's representatives and Parklands parents. On 23rd December a Mr Rogers of the Parklands School Committee had phoned me to explain that as Parklands parents had recently raised and contributed £1,900 towards the cost of erecting an assembly hall at the school, they very understandably wished to recover this money and use it to set up a scholarship fund for the school's ex-pupils. If, said Mr Rogers, Hospital Hill governors were prepared to pay this sum to his committee, he would use his influence to ensure the Parklands premises were vacated promptly so that we could move in at the beginning of the January term. The inference seemed to be that if we did not pay up, they would delay our move as long as possible.

I explained that any decisions could only be made by the board of governors, pointing out that, so close to Christmas, I expected little success in contacting them, let alone calling a meeting. As Mr Rogers was so insistent I agreed after consultation with John to attend a meeting in the office of a Mr Bromley in the Education Department next day, which was Christmas Eve, to listen to any proposals which might be made. Mr Bromley, the colonial servant, repeated Mr Rogers' suggestion of the previous day, explaining that the sum of £1,900 was about half the total cost of the hall and if Hospital Hill paid up 'the transfer could be effected more easily and rapidly'. I reiterated that I had no authority to speak for the board but that I thought it unlikely they had the resources (I knew they did not) to provide this money even if they wished to do so. How, I asked, was it possible, to buy half a building, the other half of which belonged to government and which stood on government land? And surely, I said, the Parklands parents must have been aware, given the climate of the time, of the threat of Parklands school's imminent closure? It emerged that the Treasury had promised to repay Parklands parents if Hospital Hill did not pay up – but of course both participants to that agreement would prefer to sting us.

Mrs Angus had told us that she was prepared to move at 48 hours' notice, and in the meantime had managed to arrange rental of yet another of Delamere Girls' School's classrooms. Meanwhile, the board went ahead with new admissions, secure in the belief that the school had a future. But after several more rather acrimonious exchanges between the department (which at one time attributed lack of progress to the dilatoriness of HHS's Board!), Parklands parents and Hospital Hill's governors, the move was accomplished on the 15th February. It was a superb piece of organisation by Mrs Angus and her loyal staff and for days the whole school basked in an air of festivity. Our daughter Shereen was in the top year of the school by then and still remembers the excitement of the move and the sense of responsibility she felt as she ushered younger pupils to their new classrooms.

Compensation, or separate arrangements for the use of the school hall, had not entered into the Ministry of Education's proposals for Hospital Hill's takeover of Parklands premises, and the board therefore considered the subject as closed. John put on record receiving several phone calls from members of the Education Department speaking on Mr Bromley's behalf concerning compensation for Parklands parents, and Derek Erskine commented that the whole business appeared to have been most unethical.

What I had found particularly distasteful in it all was the fact that Parklands parents and Education Department officials had deliberately targeted me, not John, to put forward their case for compensation. They had, I felt, imagined that because I had a white skin, I would instinctively feel loyalty to the all-white Parklands parents. For all their comprehension of Hospital Hill and what it stood for, we might have lived on different planets.

This had been the colonial servants' last throw. In their dealings with us they had succeeded at times in being simultaneously patronising and impertinent, but now it seemed that a golden future lay ahead for Hospital Hill School.

The school's racial mix

When John and I originally considered the concept of a multiracial school it had been apparent to us that, should we succeed in setting up a school which became educationally attractive, it could readily be swamped by children of one race. Initially that would be the Asians, then, with increasing economic power, it could be Africans. (Already well served educationally, we did not envisage such a problem with Europeans.) To guard against this, we resolved that admissions should be on the basis of one third of available places for each race. This of course did not reflect the racial composition of the country, but we were engaged in an experiment to demonstrate that only good could come from educating children of all races together. The theory was that the friendships and understanding which resulted would act as a gradual leaven throughout the general community. Given the prejudices of the colonial era we accepted that achieving such a mix would take time, but the board of governors never faltered from this ideal.

It is interesting to note that one of the most successful private schools in Kenya today, St Andrew's, Turi, originally founded more than 50 years ago as a Church of England school and now run as a trust by a board of governors, has for some years adopted this same admissions policy of parity between races. (One can speculate that had such a policy been positively followed when the first influx of black and Asian immigrants arrived in Britain, prejudice against them might have been lessened.)

In the school's early days generous support had always come from the Asian community. Without it, there would have been no school. By the early 1960s prominent and well-informed Europeans began in numbers to enrol their young, and by then there were some educated, therefore better paid – and no doubt politicised – Africans who were interested and supportive. On 21st December 1960 Tom Mboya moved a motion in Legislative Council referring to unsatisfactory answers from the temporary minister for education, John Miller, to questions the previous day about a suitable site for Hospital Hill School. Hansard reports Tom speaking at length. The main burden of his address was that 'the problem of siting could . . . have been overcome if, in fact, the Minister and the Ministry were prepared to treat this school, as indeed many of us do, as the most significant single experiment that has come out of Kenya.' That, we felt, was praise indeed.

Soon children of Jomo Kenyatta, Daniel arap Moi, Ken Matiba (the new permanent secretary in the Ministry of Education), other African politicians such as Ronald Ngala (the LegCo member from the coast), Gikonyo Kiano and Kariuki Njiri were among those of up-and-coming Africans enrolled in the school, as was Tom's elder daughter Rose. Early in 1963 Charles Njonjo, the new attorney general, became a governor of Hospital Hill.

By the second term of 1963 the full impact of the move to Parklands was demonstrated by the school's total enrolment of 266 pupils in 11 classes. The makeup by race was 118 Asians, 60 Europeans, 88 Africans. No class exceeded 25 in size. Several years before, the governors had had to deal with a possible financial crisis threatened by keeping places vacant for potential European and African applicants. They had then decided that pro tem they would admit twice as many Asian as other races, modifying this ratio each year until parity (or as near to it as was practicable) could be attained. Three years later this had been achieved, a total of 356 breaking down into 108 Asians, 118 Europeans and 130 Africans. Twenty one nationalities were represented and 50 % of the pupils were Kenyan. There is no record that year of their gender, but a year previously the enrolment of 302 had comprised 168 boys and 134 girls.

With such an excellent racial mix among the pupils, was it not high time to promote it among the teachers? Carey Francis, the great headmaster of the renowned Alliance High School for African boys, had recently retired and his place been taken by another eminent educationalist, Laurie Campbell. Campbell sent his young children to Hospital Hill and soon, for a while, became a governor. When the topic of searching for suitably qualified African teachers was broached at a board meeting, he told his slightly astonished fellow governors that none of his pupils at Alliance were planning to train as primary school teachers as their pay would be so abysmally poor. They were all heading for much more lucrative professions.

The new Government Teacher Training College for Asians at Highridge had recently produced its first qualified women, one of whom, Miss Rao, taught for a while at Hospital Hill before going on to Manchester University on a bursary. But the most pertinent comment came from Dr Samson Mwathi, a long-time governor with four children in the school. African parents, he said, did not want their children taught by teachers who did not have perfect English accents! As well as a good education, that was one of the things they paid for.

Mrs Angus had had to leave government service when she reached retirement age and it was then that she had come to Hospital Hill as headmistress. Excellent though she had been over the past six years, the governors had to look to the future. In July John had an informal discussion with her, during which she said she could not promise to continue as headmistress for a further five years and that she fully understood the board's desire for continuity during the difficult years ahead. She had suggested that if a younger man were appointed, she would be willing to continue as senior mistress under his headship. This John reported to the board on 15th July, together with his assurance to her that they would endeavour to ensure she should suffer no financial loss as a result.

After further thought, Mrs Angus had told the board she would wish to retire in the not-too-distant future, as she felt her continuing presence would be difficult both for her and the new headmaster. This was a valid assessment, and it was agreed that she should continue in post until the end of 1963, the end of the then academic year. Her decision was perhaps partly due to the realisation that Kenya was changing rapidly (in the following year she and her family returned to South Africa to live) but was chiefly influenced by an unfortunate oversight by me, and its consequences.

For any school correspondence I naturally used its stationery, which showed its own box number, altering this to our personal number where necessary. On one occasion, in a hurry I suppose but with unhappy consequences, I failed to do this when sending a brief reply, asking for his CV, to a local teacher who had contacted one of the governors about the possibility of applying for the job of headteacher. His reply, not addressed to me personally (though his letter was marked 'Confidential' and began 'Dear Mrs Karmali') but to the Honorary Secretary of the Board, was opened by Mrs Angus's secretary, who brought it to me with the smiling assurance that she had not read it. Manifestly and hardly surprisingly, this was untrue. Indeed, it soon appeared that every teacher in the school had read it. The timing was particularly unfortunate as Mrs Angus was rightly basking in the glow of the formidably complex but successful move the previous term into the new premises. Only the governors knew that at the time she was appointed she had intimated her agreement that a young headmaster was needed to ensure the school's future.

At the news of her resignation there was a surge of angry protest from anxious parents and fiercely loyal teachers. Rumours abounded. Some members of the PTA, as can so readily happen, were inclined to usurp the role of the board of governors. In answer to a letter from Richard Hughes, the PTA chairman and an ex-officio governor (who was quite clear about their respective roles), enclosing a petition signed by some teachers and parents, John took the unusual step of writing on the 25th July (in his personal capacity as there was no time to call a meeting of the board) to each parent and member of staff.

In his letter he put on record the board's need to constantly bear in mind the school's long-term future development, and that Mrs Angus had not felt able to promise to continue as head for a substantial period. Therefore it had had to look to the future and seek a new headmaster, but that there was no intention of replacing her immediately. She had been asked to reconsider and remain as headmistress at least until the end of the year. John concluded,

'The Board has no preconceived idea about the future Headmaster, except that he must be the best available.'

The affair rumbled on for some weeks. The board had a problem in commanding a quorum at its meeetings due mostly to the Education Department's dilatoriness in replacing one of its two official governors. When he was eventually appointed in November, Michael Njenga, the first African official governor, proved to be a joy and a mine of useful information about the department in which he worked. Sadly, he was to die within a very few years.

Although Kenneth Matiba, the new permanent secretary was personally sympathetic to the school's needs, he was subject to financial constraints. The emergency had drained Kenya's finances, and had it not been for the fiscal abilities and persuasive skills of its minister of finance, Sir Ernest Vasey, when dealing with the City of London, the country would undoubtedly have been bankrupt. New rules inflicted a cut in the grant-in-aid, which in the past paid 80% of teachers salaries in all grant-aided schools, to only 40%. At the same time, a new European primary school, Lavington, was most lavishly equipped by the department in stark contrast to its parsimonious response to the needs of Hospital Hill.

Finding a new headmaster

The board's meeting of 1st October was attended by Mr J D Cole-Baker, secretary of the International Schools Association of Geneva, and headmaster of the International School in Geneva. We had been in touch with him, and knowing that he was to be in East Africa for the opening of the International School of Tanganyika, the board had asked to meet him. He spoke of the implications of becoming an international school, making some helpful suggestions and offering his assistance in the search for a suitable headmaster.

In early November Richard Hughes related this to a general meeting of the PTA, adding that as a result of advertisements placed in a number of international journals, the board had decided on one name from a short list of four, chosen from 11 suitable applicants. The appointment would soon be announced of the selected candidate.

Even the most critical parents seemed to be impressed by this information, but they wanted the board to appreciate the need for more discussion and consultation with them in planning for future developments. They finally assented that the main cause of the difficulties of recent months had been that neither parents nor teachers had used the proper machinery of the parent teacher association, and it was this that had resulted in the breakdown of relationships. However, after hearing all the facts, the PTA delegation were unanimous in concluding that the board had acted with complete propriety after very careful deliberation over a considerable period. So the air was cleared. Or was it?

There had to be a scapegoat and Richard Hughes, thought to be running with the hare and the hounds since he was both PTA chairman and a governor, became the sacrificial victim. (Fortunately, he was protected by an impenetrable sense of self esteem). A small claque led by a parent, Ismail Kassam, proposed a vote of no confidence in him. An amendment was put forward and a secret ballot proposed by another parent Professor Kettle, but this was voted out by a show of hands. The subsequent open ballot carried the vote of no confidence.

A later motion on a point of order by Professor Kettle 'That if a secret ballot is requested it must be granted,' eventually reversed the vote, but by then Richard had had enough. He resigned, and thus could no longer represent the PTA on the board. As the other governors valued his contributions to the school's welfare and development he was eventually elected a governor in his own right.

The year 1964 began with a board meeting on 3rd January at

which the school's new headmaster, David King, was in attendance. The previous month at the end of term, John had written to each parent giving details about David. He came to us after four and a half years at the International School of Geneva where he had specialised in the instruction of English and maths, but was also qualified to teach history, geography, nature study, music, art, physical education and Latin – a formidable array. Bearing in mind that his pupils had largely been children of diplomats, United Nations staff and similarly well-paid and presumably discerning people, his credentials were impressive. Why, one might ask, did he decide to leave such desirable surroundings? The answer seemed to be the lure of Africa and pastures new, plus the challenge of a school like Hospital Hill.

On their arrival on 31st December, David and his family had moved into the headmaster's house in the Parklands school compound. They had been particularly welcomed by a fellow Scot, Anne Innes, a dedicated, charming, and competent teacher who had joined the staff the previous May. She was an enormous help to them in settling in and finding their feet in new surroundings, though we too had gone out of our way to make them especially welcome. Although it was 17 years since our arrival in Kenya, I still remembered my initial bewilderment at the sudden change in lifestyles.

Several members of staff who felt particular loyalty to Mrs Angus had resigned, but good replacements had been found. Even Gloria Hagberg, due for overseas leave in May, had indicated that she would prefer to be relieved of her post before that. David King was assured that he had the full backing of the board in any tightening of discipline.

David, in his 30s, exuded energy, enthusiasm and competence. John and I felt that with such a man in charge of the school we could at last relax and allow other interests a place in our lives. I had found work for the school in recent years very time-consuming and was also unhappy at the acrimony and general nastiness which had been unleashed by my error over the post office box number, so I intimated at this meeting that I wished to stand down as honorary secretary to the board.

In view of the expected reduction of grant-in-aid, fees were to be raised to 280 shillings per term, as in all city council schools receiving such aid from the local authority, but parents generally were not unhappy about the increase. There was such a 'family' feeling in the school that the PTA was already raising funds for a bursary scheme to help those children in school whose parents could not afford the additional sum.

Ben Miles, a government servant who had been an outstandingly sympathetic and helpful official governor, proposed at this meeting that an executive committee should be appointed from among board members to consider matters of general policy. Ben himself, Michael Njenga, Ronald Dain and Kersie Moddie were elected, under John's chairmanship, David King to act as secretary. The creation of this smaller, more committed core body augured well for faster action over issues which might arise in future.

The following month David King told the executive committee meeting that after a talk with two teachers who had failed to show the co-operation he looked for in his staff, they had both handed in their resignations, finishing at the school the previous week. He had replaced them without difficulty, one new recruit being Miss Lalani, a newly qualified High Ridge trainee, who was also an experienced Girl Guider. She would work next door to Mrs Ayerst, a highly competent teacher. Another new recruit was experienced in training junior choirs, which would be a new area of expertise for Hospital Hill.

David's comprehensive overview indicated not only that he was already on top of the job but that a new era in the life of the school was about to begin.

147

The breaking down of other racial barriers

All these exciting changes at Hospital Hill were set in the context of even more gripping and challenging events in the country as a whole. We had learnt from personal experience that there were racially-tolerant whites in the country, but while the climate was dominated by a vociferous self-seeking section of Europeans, it took real character to come out against those opinions. Only a few did so, notably, in our experience, the Erskines, the Vaseys, and the Reiss family, who so courageously pioneered white enrolment in Kenya's only multiracial school.

As mentioned earlier, when the British Labour government had appointed Richard Frost as the British Council's first representative in Kenya in 1947, over and above the Council's traditional role of promoting British culture Frost was entrusted with the task of improving race relations. This he sincerely attempted, his home being one of the few of the time where party guests regularly included members of all three races. But his upper-middle class, public school and Oxbridge background (and the more than ordinarily plummy tones of his admirable wife Tam) made many non-whites suspicious and he seems to have had little contact with the most dynamic African politicians such as Mboya and Argwings-Kodhek. Although Dick became one of Hospital Hill's first governors and was always encouraging, he did not send his own children there. But that was understandable since their stay in Kenya was temporary and they needed to remain in the British system. (Notably, his successor as British Council representative, Sandy Ross and his wife Eve, showed no hesitation in sending their young daughter Margaret to Hospital Hill.)

It was notable that during our time in Kenya any friendships we made with British officials were almost invariably with those from the British Council and they often showed interest in Hospital Hill School. With one or two exceptions (the de Frietas's, the Pecks and the Duffs,) we found few kindred spirits among British

High Commissioners and their staffs, who mainly shared the outlook of white settlers and enjoyed associating with those who might be considered 'uppercrust'.

Although resolved to undermine the accepted racial prejudices of the country, John had been equally determined not to expose me to petty unpleasantnesses. We had never, for instance, attempted to enter the big hotels. But in 1950 we had been foolish enough to allow white friends, Steven Hubbard, principal of the East African Posts and Telegraph's training school in Langata, and his wife Agnes, to persuade us to go dancing with them at the Salisbury hotel in the Westlands area of Nairobi, where, Steve was convinced, no objections would be raised – he had checked with the management. He was wrong. Halfway through the first dance, the band-leader stopped Steve and me, took him aside, and said 'Get that Indian off the floor or the band will refuse to play'. This, within five years of world-wide revulsion at revelations of the horrors of the Holocaust, was particularly bizarre, since the bandleader was himself Jewish. (A case of 'little fleas have lesser fleas …'?) Poor Steve was mortified on our behalf, even more upset than we. Agi, herself Jewish, was almost incandescent with rage. We withdrew in good order. Not until about 1960, with the perception that independence was inevitable, even imminent, did Asians and Africans begin to patronise – to be tolerated in – the big hotels and restaurants.

As early as 1953 the Hotel Keepers Association agreed to abolish the colour bar in their establishments, but this was largely ignored by white owners and managers, especially in the white highlands and at the coast. As late as 1959 the tyres of Tom Mboya's car were slashed outside the Outspan Hotel in Nyeri where he was staying as part of a group of fact-finding LegCo backbenchers, which included whites.

Regiments of the British army were sent to Kenya during the Mau Mau emergency to augment the police and all-white Kenya Regiment in suppressing the unrest, and it is significant that many of its soldiers were appalled and amazed at the European settlers' arrogance, which they were to witness on many occasions. Why, some of them wondered, were they sent to Kenya to help perpetuate such a privileged way of life? The centre seemed to be cracking. Surely things would fall apart?

John and I could take stock of the crusade we had determined on when I agreed to marry him and go to live in Kenya. We were not aggressive warriors against the colour bar, believing at first that we might progress by example. By this I do not mean that we necessarily wished to encourage inter-racial marriage, merely that if two people fell in love across the colour divide, they should not feel doomed. Neither should it be assumed that their offspring would feel rejected by both races and therefore, as 'half-castes', that odious and now outmoded term, be considered in any way as inferior human beings. If in the past some of them had felt themselves misfits we considered that to be not their fault but the fault of society. And society could be changed. Our attitude was positive. We should attempt to give our children experience of the best of both worlds. My acceptance by the Ismaili community had flown in the face of what was then the received wisdom.

To anyone with any knowledge of history it was evident that nations and tribes had intermingled and intermarried – if sometimes involuntarily – for as long as humanity had existed. John and I felt the flow of history was with us and such mixing would continue to evolve, with increasing acceleration as the world's populations became more mobile.

It was soon clear that that meant nothing in the Kenya context. But we had, through dogged determination, been largely instrumental in establishing the first, and for ten years the only, multiracial school. The opinion occasionally voiced, that we started Hospital Hill only to provide an education for our own children was not entirely accurate. It had indeed solved our personal problem and without that impetus it is unlikely we should have found the energy to put into the project. Nevertheless although our last child left at the end of 1963 we were determined never to give up on the school's future and John remained as a dedicated and hard-hitting chairman of its board until the closing chapter in 1973. His name was a golden thread which ran from beginning to end, through the rainbow tapestry of Hospital Hill's history.

Our failure to provide a similar secondary school was a bitter blow, but the project had proved both too expensive and too contentious politically. The very success of Hospital Hill scared most of the white community to death and they were determined to delay any extension of multiracial education.

Our second chemist's shop

All this went on while we were working to build up our business so that we could afford decent further education for our children. The Block family in the aftermath of the war determined to expand their business interests. They owned the New Stanley and Norfolk Hotels in Nairobi, managed the hugely popular Nyali Beach Hotel in Mombasa and the Sinbad in Malindi, and also had farming interests up-country. A facelift for the New Stanley was decided upon. By then, late 1958, we were well established as a pharmacy and photographic business in our large premises in Hardinge Street, close to what was a city car park and is now the site of the Hilton Hotel.

Jack Block, whom we had met briefly at a party at the home of Derek Erskine's daughter Petal Harragin, wandered into the shop one day, ostensibly to buy a film. Chatting to John, he spoke of his plans for the New Stanley which provided for the incorporation of six small shops, and casually asked if we might be interested in renting one of them as a pharmacy. We certainly should, for in those days the New Stanley was at the hub of Nairobi, its windows

151

looking out on to what became a contentious statue of Lord Delamere. (This was banished after independence to his family farm at Elmenteita, where it pensively gazes out over the land he had loved.)

In October 1959 we opened in the tiny shop in the modernised New Stanley, which was too small to carry a full range of prescription medicines, so some of these had to be sent down to the Hardinge Street shop to be dispensed. But service was swift. Our pharmacist there was under instruction to give them reasonable priority and few people had to wait more than ten minutes for their medicines. The Blocks just wanted their clients to have ready access to a chemists shop and most of our customers were in search of films, painkillers, anti-malarials, remedies for upset tummies, suntan lotion and the like.

Initially, I ran that shop, which looked out on to the famous Thorn Tree outdoor coffee shop. Itinerant hippies and other sixties travellers left messages for each other pinned to the thorn tree's bark. John remained a hundred yards or so away in the Hardinge Street shop. Before long he freed me by taking over the New Stanley shop in the afternoons. It was his photographic expertise which became the great draw for those tourists who, having bought or been given an unfamiliar camera for their once-in-a-lifetime safari holiday, found themselves unable to operate it. We have lost count of the famous and infamous who dealt with us, but numbered among them were Louis Armstrong (and all his band), Robert Ruark, Grace Kelly, Frank Sinatra, Clark Gable – and Princess Marina of Kent, though rather than staying at the hotel she was the personal guest of Jack and Doria Block in their luxurious Muthaiga home.

Taking on the racists in other social arenas

John had determined to lay siege to other mono-racial organisations in Kenya, including the Rotary Movement and the bodies which ran sports. Victor Browse ran a successful opticians business in Nairobi. Originally from South Africa, he was Jewish and an old acquaintance of K's. Although it was to be many years before we were invited to his house, he was friendly towards us from our early days in the city, and would frequently engage me in conversation when I happened to be passing his shop.

The iniquities of racial segregation often came up and Vic was particularly critical of Nairobi Rotary Club, of which he was a member, and whose motto was 'Service Before Self'. The organisation, which is of course international, also embraced the principle of 'fellowship among men'. In Kenya, it appeared, it was alright to demonstrate fellowship among men of all races in Mombasa (was it that relaxing and enervating climate?), but in Nairobi only whites were eligible.

Seeing John as qualified by character and education to become a member of Nairobi Rotary (in theory only the most eminent in their profession or business in any location would be considered), Vic began lobbying behind the scenes for his election. Every time, he reported, John was blackballed. This did not break John's heart since he was not at all sure he wished to spend valuable time hobnobbing with men most of whose outlook and values so differed from his own. But it was a matter of principle so he made no objection to Vic's campaign, which was also supported by Sir Charles Mortimer. Doria Block's mother was a sister of Vic Browse and we later learned that it was Vic who had assured Jack that we were the best and most efficient pharmacists in Nairobi and should be offered the New Stanley shop.

Eventually, many years later, John, together with his cousin Shamsu Ahamed and a Sikh, Kirpal Singh Sagoo, were elected to the Nairobi club. One of its prominent white members resigned in protest and left Kenya to live in South Africa.

As a youth John had belonged to the Aga Khan Club in Parklands, mainly a sports club. Here, during a long period of convalescence after barely surviving a bout of blackwater fever, he had honed his skills at billiards. On his return he rejoined the club, where he played tennis and in due course, was elected its chairman.

The club committee resolved to host a dinner for those of its members who had distinguished themselves in various sports, and to which they invited a number of prominent non-Ismaili sportsmen. One of these was the eminent Sikh chairman of the Asian Sports Associaton, Mahan Singh. Like John, he was a small brown man (though in his case, bearded and turbanned) whose appearance belied the force of their personalities. The usual competitiveness, wheeler-dealing and jealousies animated the Kenyan sports world as in others, but Mahan Singh, an honest and determined man, had welded the organisation into an effective body. He was greatly respected in the whole Asian community and on good terms with his European counterparts. But now he was tired, and after seeing John in action at the sports dinner, he approached him and suggested John take over from him in the Asian Sports Association, which duly happened.

This led to John, along with Mahan Singh, becoming a member of the Kenya Olympic Association, of which the president was Brigadier General Sir Godfrey Rhodes. By then retired, Sir Godfrey had been general manager of the Kenya and Uganda Railways. A liberal-minded man with a longstanding knowledge of Kenya, he made innumerable, largely unheralded contributions to racial understanding in the country. In addition to being president of the Hockey Union of Kenya, Sir Godrey was chief scout, and involved in the St John's Ambulance Brigade, two areas of Kenya life where membership was open to all races.

The Kenya hockey team, consisting almost entirely of Asians, with one or two European players, was already of a very high standard, and international tours were organised. When the outstandingly talented Pakistani team visited Kenya, I recall tension running high at matches where some Kenyans preferred to support the visitors rather than their home side which had some white players. It was a genial and authoritative Sir Godfrey, with his imposing height and great tact, who always managed to lower the temperature and, with the help of officials, restore order.

As the wife of the president of the Asian Sports Association I was once invited to sit with officials of the Kenya Cricket Association (Europeans only) and their wives, to watch a match between a Kenya side and a visiting team from what was then Southern Rhodesia. The ladies were charming and welcomed me kindly. I sat with them in their reserved enclosure for what I anticipated would be a pleasant afternoon. Believing that I was tuned in to European attitudes in the country, I was nonetheless surprised to hear my companions rooting for the white Rhodesians, not the brown Kenya team.

At that period in its history the concept of 'Kenya' claimed no loyalty from either the white or brown races. It was 'home' to only black Africans, who had nowhere else to go. Among their leaders, only Tom Mboya had a vision of eliminating tribalism and establishing a united nation, which began to happen in his and Kenyatta's day, but seems to be rapidly disintegrating under the present leadership.

Once elected chairman of the Asian Sports Association, John determined to begin eliminating racial divisions in the sports world. He wrote to the Football Association of Kenya suggesting that its Europeans-only membership should be widened to include all races, having in mind particularly the African population which was already demonstrating a significant talent for the game.

As a result he received an official invitation to a meeting held in the whites-only Railway Club and asked to put his case. As he concluded and sat down, a European representing the army rose

155

to his feet, stood to conspicuous attention and said 'We, the British, have ruled the British Empire for centuries and we have no intention of giving up control of football in this colony!'. That about summed up the feeling of the meeting, but John was not discouraged, knowing he had struck the first blow in what was likely to be a long campaign.

Having acquired his first 35mm camera with most of our wedding present money, John became a keen photographer. No children ever suffered so many photocalls as ours did. While we still lived in London he entered and occasionally won competitions set in the *Amateur Photographer* magazine. Kenya offered wider opportunities for landscape photography and with the additional asset of a Leica camera some of his work was extremely good. But when he attempted to exhibit his pictures in the photographic section of the Kenya Arts and Crafts Society's annual exhibition, he was barred. Sorry, Mr Karmali, your skin's the wrong colour.

Dick Frost was so incensed when he heard this that he exercised his right as a society member and displayed John's work as 'sponsored by the British Council'. An interesting sidelight on this affair is that the intransigent chairman of the Kenya Arts and Crafts Society at the time was a Mrs Lulu Dyer, of the same military family as the General Dyer who had been responsible for the infamous Amritsar massacre. Racial prejudice can be nurtured in the bosom of a family, clearly for generations.

The bastion of white memsahib opinion in Kenya was the mis-leadingly named East African Women's League, the EAWL. EAWWL would have been a more accurate acronym – East African White Women's League. They were almost vicious in their opposition to any form of racial integration. At least one letter appeared in *The East African Standard* deploring the fact that the writer had seen from her car several little blonde children sitting on the grass verges of the road with their black ayahs. How tragic, it was suggested, that such innocent tots should be thus exposed to the degrading influence of primitive Africans.

There was no way in which I would be persuaded to take on such viragos. Apart from guarding the moral state of the white inhabitants of Kenya, their main interest was in the domestic arts, and while I could admire some of their work, their jams, cakes, and embroidery, it was not my scene even if I had been able to find the occasional kindred spirit.

Some years later Verry Vasey told me that when he was minister for education and the local papers first carried the story of possible government money for Hospital Hill School, a deputation from the EAWL, led by its then chairman, a certain Lady Sydney Farrar, had waited upon him to seek an assurance that no more government support would be considered for multiracial education. It was an assurance he had felt unable to give – but I'm sure he conveyed the sad news with his usual charm and tact.

That is not to say that the EAWL did no good work. Among other things, the organisation did exert pressure on the government which lead to the passing of an Adoption Act, one benefit of which was that a child's name could then be added to an adoptive parent's passport.

A social embarrassment

I must wryly relate one occasion when I felt the EAWL ladies might have had the edge over me. During the period in the 1950s when we got to know members of the Baring 'court', we were one day invited to lunch at Government House. Wearing a smart silk suit and small feathered hat, quite *comme il faut*, I found myself sitting on the governor's right. It was a small party of about eight people, one of whom was the British MP and minister, John Profumo, later to achieve a certain notoriety.

Sir Evelyn, who had clearly heard about us and the school (and possibly knew that it was I who made his pills) was at pains to put me at ease, chatting about his previous experiences in India and

South Africa. Suddenly on my left a silver dish was being proffered – containing artichokes. I have to say that during the 1930s in Rhyl and later in wartime England, artichokes had not been greatly in evidence, and I had not one clue about how to tackle them. Suppressing panic, I waved the servant away, and was then condemned to sit for what seemed forever while everyone else enjoyed their delicious starter. I should of course, have merrily confessed my ignorance to Sir Evelyn and sought his guidance. For long after I squirmed at the memory and had to dig deep to resurrect my sense of humour. EAWL ladies, I felt sure, would not have been so embarrassingly discommoded.

Other activities

Both music and drama escaped the pervading racial divide, and in this field Dick Frost successfully initiated annual music and drama festivals with British Council sponsorship. After Shereen became a boarder at Kenya High School for Girls and the boys were overseas, I went back to my first love, acting, and won an award as the best supporting actress, playing Jocasta in an Asian Group's production of Oedipus Rex. The professional adjudicator commented that had I had better direction he would have placed me first. On the strength of that I won a role in a production of *Six Characters in Search of an Author* under Robert Beaumont's direction. But though I loved acting, the long and late hours at the National Theatre and the lonely drive home, often in the early hours, convinced me that I must seek other outlets for my energies. (This I eventually did by involvement as a 'Friend' of a children's Home run by the Salvation Army, an organisation for which I acquired great respect; and with the Kenya Museum Society, which, over the years, has contributed much to the National Museums, including the organisation of the Know Kenya Course which runs till this day).

As it became clear that all schools and indeed every other organisation would be required to cease the practice of segregation when independence came – and that would be soon – efforts were made to admit some suitable non-white children to the European secondary schools. Notably, Miss Janette Stott, appointed head-mistress of Kenya Girls High in 1942, was liberally inclined and believed that it would be easier to integrate education for girls than for boys, on the basis that girls were more likely to discuss domestic and non-controversial matters, while boys usually discussed politics! Frost records the careful and gradual manner in which she paved the way for the introduction of her policy of accepting some Asian girls into sixth form science classes at Kenya High, and how it was scuppered by the ladies of the East African Women's League. (The Asian girls' schools were less well-endowed and so too poorly equipped to teach sixth form science.)

In those days the system whereby aldermen were part of local government still existed. They were appointed by an electoral college of councillors elected by their own racial electorate. In the early 1960s John became an alderman of Nairobi City Council and on afternoons when he had committee meetings I stayed in town to look after the New Stanley shop.

Not all John's energies went into the crusade against racialism. In the late 1940s, soon after our own arrival, Mollie and Donovan Maule came to Nairobi. Both actors from a long acting tradition and of an older generation than us, they had spent the war entertaining troops in various parts of the world. They were to create a small club theatre in Nairobi, the Donovan Maule Theatre, which began its life above a grocer's shop in Government Road, opposite what is now the Kenya Cinema. Coming from cosmo-politan Cairo, they had no thought of restricting their audiences to 'whites only', and, missing theatre more than most things, we became two of the theatre's earliest members.

Chatting with John one day, Don mused on the need for greater

159

publicity for his theatre. He had persuaded various shops and clubs to display small frames of photographs of current productions. From then on for many years, John spent the evenings – and often much of the nights – of the Maule's dress rehearsals taking publicity photos, both of individual actors and of scenes from the plays.

At times I went too. We loved the relaxed and friendly atmosphere of the theatre and made a number of friendships among the actors and actresses, the most valued and lasting of which was that with the lovely redhead Loretta Davitt, who came out from the Bristol Old Vic in 1956 to play Sabrina in *Sabrina Fair*, and the man she met on the plane who eventually became her husband, Michael Tremlett. They have been 'family' ever since. When they married in late 1957 John gave Loretta away (he was getting quite accustomed to this job!); Shereen was Loretta's small flower girl, and we held a wedding reception for them in our garden at Speke Road. Some 30 years later when the Tremlett's daughter Caroline married, things came full circle and Shereen's daughter Kainde was a flower girl.

A multi-racial school in an independent country

As David King began his determined endeavours to bring Hospital Hill's standards up to the best he had known in Europe, the Parent Teacher Association, which had been so rent by the Mrs Angus affair, elected a new chairman, Marjean Bailey. Her husband, the Reverend Jack Bailey, had recently been appointed to a lecturer's post at St Paul's Theological College in Limuru, some 20 miles and several thousand feet beyond Nairobi – in the white highlands in fact.

Marjean herself was well on the way to becoming an ordained priest (she and Jack had met while students at Columbia) but had given up her studies to devote herself to her husband and what was by now a family of three children. But her phenomenal energies were by no means exhausted by these commitments. When they learnt that there was just one school in Kenya which was not racially segregated, the Baileys had no doubts at all.

A 20 mile trip, often four times a day, was nothing compared to the psychological harm their children might suffer if raised in a racist, therefore un-Christian, whites-only, ambience. Amadea, Adam, and Saskia were duly enrolled at Hospital Hill. Their parents threw themselves into fund-raising and other supportive activities at the school, along with all the other dedicated parents. A library fund was quickly set up, and possible changes in the school's uniform discussed, something less formal. And how about a swimming pool?

Another most welcome factor in the school's favour was the appearance in the Ministry of Education, dealing with Hospital Hill affairs, of a colonial servant who actually thought multiracial education was a good thing. J. Roger Carter, brother of the then vice-chancellor of Lancaster University, had been active in the search for a new headmaster. Writing to a colleague in the Ministry of Education in London who had been helpful with advice, he remarked that David King looked like being 'an exceptionally good Headmaster', adding the hope that he 'will make a really good thing of Hospital Hill and enable it to play the part for which it is so clearly cut out'.

Carter was later to bring to King's attention that the school's establishment was not being fully utilised, and that he could in fact employ one more member of staff, relieving him of the responsibility of full time teaching of the top class, standard VII, and thus releasing him to devote more time to reorganising the school's administration to its best advantage. Roger Carter was a true friend to Hospital Hill – why had we not met him before? Because, I would guess, until independence loomed, he, as one of the more able civil servants, had been allocated to matters

161

concerning European education only. But that is only surmise.

David lost no time in identifying two areas of need. (He had quickly modified the old system, sanctioned by the Education Department for all primary schools, whereby European teachers had two afternoons off a week.) Although he was more than capable of supervising sports, the school required something more, a man who could devote more time and energy to it. With the assistance of Desmond Cole-Baker in Geneva, he was able to recruit a former colleague from the international school there. Stanley French arrived early in 1965 to take up the post of sports and social studies teacher.

The other need which became apparent in due course was for a teacher who could deal with children with special needs, some-times in coping with the English language. Gloria Hagberg, already back in Nairobi (Gordon now headed the Kenya office of the International Institute for Education), with her warm and outgoing nature seemed ideal for the task and was appointed. With a gap of four years (1967–1971) when Gordon was trans-ferred to the Washington office, Gloria taught in the school until the age of 65, retiring in 1978 after several years as deputy head – but that comes later in the story.

'Social studies' and 'special needs'! Were these not esoteric additions to Hospital Hill's curriculum? Desmond Cole-Baker and David King had both discussed with the board at different times the desirability of the school becoming, officially, an international school. Enquiries from the managing director of Esso among other prominent business people in the city, par-ticularly Americans, had prompted such a consideration. Quite what the objections were is not now clear, but they seemed to hinge on a fear that such a move, presumably because of the potential to increase fees, might jeopardise the future of Kenyans, lower paid than expatriates, in the school. Since this was the total antithesis of its ethos, the idea of such an official move was rejected, but both Cole-Baker and King urged the desirability of becoming in essence not a national, but an 'international' school, by adopting a sufficiently flexible curriculum to enable pupils to enter any subsequent educational system.

Early in the year the board submitted through Roger Carter a memorandum to the recently appointed Education Commission, recording their own experience in running a multiracial school, emphasising the need for small classes and a high quality of teacher. These were the factors, together with the broadening of the syllabus which David found desirable, which put the fees of Hospital Hill a little above those in city council schools. The memo continued, 'To most parents Hospital Hill School has meant more than just a school their children attend for education.' They felt that by sending them to a multiracial school 'they were contributing towards establishing a new integrated society which the new Kenya needs'. They were therefore ready to pay something over the odds, but all recognised the need to subsidise, by government grant or a bursary scheme, the fees of poorer parents, who would mainly be African Kenyans. For many years, the Motor Mart Trust had in fact provided bursaries to African pupils, but that trust was soon to be wound up.

This was predominantly a time of great hope for the future, both for the country and the school. Independence from Britain was achieved for Kenya on 12th December 1963 when, in the presence of its new President Jomo Kenyatta, the Duke of Edinburgh, and tens of thousands of enthusiastic members of the populace, the Union Jack was lowered and Kenya's new flag raised.

Unfortunately, though invited, we were not among those present. John had a week or so previously undergone an operation on a knee and was still confined to bed. Shereen was taken to the celebrations in a car of Tom Mboya's along with her friend Rehanna Rattansi (Hassan and Gulie's daughter), but our view of the ceremonies and firework display was confined to watching on television. But that was fun. Our home in Speke Road bordered on the African reserve and the family who owned the *duka* (shop) just beyond our boundary came to share it, sitting on cushions on the floor around John's bed, where we drank a toast to Kenya's future prosperity.

One sour note was struck near the end of the year. A young local journalist, Nick Russell, visited the school and produced an excellent article about it in *The East African Standard*, referring to it as a 'great educational experiment'. Inevitably there were some minor inaccuracies since he wrote of what he saw, and knew little of what had gone before.

Oliver Knowles wrote to the *Standard* pointing out that before David King's advent, Mrs Angus had contributed greatly to the school's success 'since its inception'. Since this was yet another small inaccuracy, John then wrote to the paper on 20th November, endorsing Knowles's praise of Mrs Angus and taking the opportunity to pay tribute to former head teachers, Nelda Welle and Margaret Porter. But the school, he wrote, had only become Hospital Hill School , and truly multiracial, in late 1953 with the move to new premises and Mrs Eileen Walke's advent as headmistress. She it was who had had to cope with the problems and prejudices which faced the school in its early days, and it was she who should be especially credited with establishing the happy atmosphere and lively spirit 'which exists in the school to this day'.

Up in Njoro, Nelda, now Mrs Kroll, felt her hackles rise. A complex character and a high-profile Christian, she was clearly an idealist, a strange mixture of one who seems to desire anonymity and yet longs for public recognition. At no time during her stint running the Co-Racial School did she tell us the names of the friends she later praised for all the help they had given her. And only three weeks before her departure had we been told of her plan to marry and leave Nairobi and the school. There was no real rapport between us, even though we shared the same aims.

Now she found it unbearable that others should receive any

recognition for the development of Hospital Hill, and on the 22nd November poured out her ire to the *Standard*. She had in fact written two weeks earlier to the editor of *The Sunday Post*, accusing us of 'self-glorification' and asserting that I had gone to the UK in the previous year with the specific intention of publicising our role in the British press. In fact, anything appearing in the overseas press was based on what their journalists had seen for themselves at the school and at no time did John or I have any contact with them. Nelda remarks casually that 'now the school was put under a Board of Governors', choosing to ignore the fact that it was John who had instigated this and that it was through his efforts and those of others that the school was now in large and more suitable premises. *The Sunday Post* editor invited John to his office to show him Nelda's letters, feeling them too libellous to publish.

In response to the *Standard* letters, John wrote dispassionately, giving chapter and verse on the school's inception and development. He ended his letter, 'I have never claimed to be the sole founder of the School, but I am the one person who has been intimately connected with its development from August 1949 to the present day.' The final comment came from Hassan Nathoo, a parent whose child had been one of the first pupils, very properly recording the contribution made by other Asians to the funding and success of the school, and with that, the correspondence closed.

Financial support from the Americans

It was a time of great excitement, a time of elation. At last Hospital Hill had a permanent home, a first-class headmaster, increasing enrolment and a supportive PTA dedicated to raising funds for extra-curricular activities. Samson Mwathi, a long-time governor, hoped to form a panel with three doctor friends whose children were pupils, so that in an emergency, medical aid should always be readily available. Richard Hughes approached the Art Society for an art teacher to attend on two afternoons a week, and a similar arrangement with the Conservatoire of Music ensured that music and some private piano lessons would also be available.

At independence responsibility for primary education in the whole country had devolved from the ministry to the local authorities. Both Tom Mboya and Charles Njonjo believed that a school like Hospital Hill would be exempt, meriting a place within the ministry's ambit because of its special ethos. When it became clear that this would not be so we still fondly believed some leeway would be accorded us.

Joel Wanyoike, the new city council education officer, a decent and educated man, seemed at first to appreciate that in view of the rather broader syllabus Hospital Hill provided, there was a need to charge slightly higher fees than other city primary schools. It was even agreed eventually that the authority would pay full grant-in-aid towards the unusually high salary (high for a primary school head, that is) which, as a graduate, David King naturally commanded. But Wanyoike's council colleagues had other views and the board was soon forced to lower the fee of 280 shillings per term it had set in January 1964 to the level of other council schools, at 250 shillings. We noted wryly that the International School of Tanzania charged fees of 600 shillings per term.

At the end of that first year under David King's headship, Hospital Hill came third out of 72 city council schools in the Kenya Preliminary Examinations, which determined a pupil's future passage to secondary education. All our dreams seemed to be coming to fruition – but we were eventually to discover that there was a worm in the bud.

The American ambassador of the time sent his child to Hospital Hill and, possibly through the good offices of Gordon Hagberg, Jim Ruchti, counselor of the embassy, contacted John, expressing interest in the school's future. 'Perhaps we can review the situation [at the end of August],' he wrote, 'including the issue of an American on your Board, finances, and next procedural steps.'

As early as June 1965 a grant of $10,000 was made to enable David to buy school materials, and though it was stipulated that this money should be spent in America it was conceded that some exceptions could be made if specific books of English origin were deemed necessary. David was delighted.

When the review mentioned by Jim Ruchti eventually took place, it resulted in Gordon Hagberg being appointed to the board of governors, Gloria's re-appointment to the staff, with particular responsibility for children with special needs (though she also taught English to the higher classes), and a grant of $38,000. Ten thousand dollars of this was partly towards the cost of the new teacher, and $28,000 to provide for the building of extra class-rooms. No strings were attached to this generous offer. It was made, the Americans said, because of the school's character and its high standard of education, which made it suitable for American children of primary age in the country.

By now a second architect, Kersie Moddie, a young Parsee with daughters in the school, was a governor, and he and Richard Hughes were entrusted with drawing up plans for the new classrooms. They took an overview, thinking in terms of re-developing the school as a whole, keeping in mind improving the standard of the present rundown quarters for maintenance staff, toilets, and some classrooms. Some of the latter were in temporary buildings and should eventually be taken down. (In 1994 they were still in use.) An infant block of six rooms, the governors decided, would accommodate Standards I and II in a three-stream school, and this should be the first phase of development.

News of American generosity had percolated through the parent community and the PTA wrote to the board asking if there were any objections to their going ahead with projects to raise money for a swimming pool. Far from it. Space for such a pool would be kept in mind when designing the new block.

Then arose the first sign of possible trouble ahead. In view of the ambitious building programme and the investment it entailed, the fact that the land on which the school was situated belonged to the government and not to the board of governors could be a problem. The board applied to the Ministry of Education for the land title to be transferred to them, but without success. Land and its possession has always been the most sensitive political issue in Kenya.

Plans were made for Charles Njonjo and John to meet the President to present the school's case. This meeting, unsurprisingly, never took place, but John was able to report to the board meeting on 26th July 1965 that he had had a letter from the ministry stating that the grounds had been given to the school 'for all times'. This was later recorded as 'a 99 years lease on the 9.66 acres occupied by the school, as long as the buildings were used as a "public school"'.

Late in 1967 David King remarked on his difficulty in finding enough suitable infant teachers for the proposed expansion and this, together with a realisation of what the building would cost, contributed to the decision that the first phase should consist of only four classrooms. As Kersie Moddie was employed by the city council, all plans emanated from Richard's office. He also handled dealings with USAID, which would pay the bills, and there was lengthy correspondence on the suitability of his plans. He had to justify his design which USAID had queried, by explaining that the space would be used by small children sitting in groups on chairs round tables, and not in rows as in a conventional classroom.

The new infant classrooms, having actually been in use since the beginning of the year, were officially opened on 11th May 1968 by the American Ambassador Glenn Fergusson, whose three children were among the school's pupils. Kersie Moddie had organised the little ceremony, and was thanked for the many ways in which he had contributed towards the scheme's success.

A swimming pool for the school

This visible sign of successful expansion stimulated the PTA to even keener fundraising efforts. In September, with £1,635 already in their swimming pool fund, they proposed four main activities to raise at least another £2,000. There was to be a motor car treasure hunt, a garden fete, a swimming gala (at a venue to be announced. Any one like to offer their pool?), a dance, and a scheme, 'proposed by that famous poet, Anonymous', whereby various parents would make cookies and candies to be sold, with David's permission, perhaps once a fortnight at playtime. They were also producing a school magazine. By February 1970, David King informed the board that the fund then stood at £4,200, and that estimates for building the pool had been sought, ranging from £6,500 to £9,000.

Some years earlier I had roped in my old friend Rahematali Abdulla, from Aga Khan Education Board days, to advise on Hospital Hill's finances, and his firm had for some time been its professional accountants. His wife was a Nimji, of the prominent Ismaili family which owned the Pioneer Insurance Company. Their children and other Nimjis were pupils, and the company now offered the PTA a loan to enable an early start to be made in constructing the pool. The only condition was that some parents should act as guarantors. This proposal was cautiously received by the board, which asked for more assurances on several aspects, such as, how did the PTA propose to service and pay for the maintenance of the pool, what safety precautions were envisaged, and what did they think could be done if any guarantors defaulted?

Presumably, these doubts were all resolved satisfactorily. (A fee for each child using the pool, of ten shillings per term seemed not excessive in ensuring its maintenance and safety.) On 23rd November that year, the pool was officially opened by John, who whenever his term of office expired, had resigned as required by the school's constitution, but always been re-elected as chairman of the board of governors. He also had another announcement to make: David King, less than happy at what he referred to as the 'make-do' attitude of the city council, was feeling restless and talking very seriously of moving on.

The parents and teachers, in particular the sports master, Stanley French, had fought and worked with enormous dedication to provide the present pupils of Hospital Hill with a swimming pool. It was an invaluable gift, not only then but also for future generations of Nairobi school children. Soon after it came into use, Hospital Hill soared to the top of the winners lists in the various swimming competitions, and this ascendancy has been maintained ever since. The school is often overtaken nowadays by teams from the many well-funded private schools, but is always near the top and remains supreme among the pupils of city council schools.

There had for some time been indications from American sources that a multiracial secondary school was desirable to which Hospital Hill's pupils could proceed. Nothing new in that idea – and if the Americans were interested, maybe the relatively enor-mous sums of money needed could be found. David King had in fact accepted the post of headmaster of Hospital Hill in the hope that such a development would occur. He was eminently qualified to take the school forward in that direction.

Kersie Moddie was asked by the board to do some research. He reported that a 12½ acre plot on the Thika Road was available for the school at a cost of £750 (which seems extraordinarily cheap), and that a group of parents including himself felt that the school should go ahead and buy it 'in spite of the debt owed to the City Council'. In the meantime he suggested that temporary buildings should be erected on the primary school site so that a Form 1 could be started at the beginning of the new year, 1971.

But rumour had it that the Highridge Teacher Training College was to be moved further out of Nairobi to more commodious premises. Could we possibly take that over as a secondary school? (This proved to be a false rumour). In fact, there were still more than enough problems with the primary school, which should surely be solved first.

A question of school fees

In the late 1960s and the early years of the 1970s the fortunes of Hospital Hill went up and down like a yo-yo. Governors departed and new governors came. Derek Erskine, who had been sufficiently sincere in his non-racist beliefs to offer hospitality in Nairobi – and pretty luxurious hospitality at that – to Jomo Kenyatta when he was first released from detention, became close to the old man. He was appointed to the boards of the country's two main secondary schools in the city, made chief whip of the Kanu African National Party (KANU), and was already involved in the multiracial arena of sports bodies and the Olympic movement. Ronald Dain similarly indicated that under the new conditions of independence he was overwhelmed by other commitments. Both men in their different ways had served Hospital Hill well, always enormously supportive, making useful contributions during the difficult days, but it was time for change.

Gordon Hagberg, the American representative on the board, was transferred to the Washington office of his organisation and was replaced as the American governor by Wendell Coote, counsellor at the embassy and equally dedicated to the advancement of the school. Sam Waruhiu, lawyer son of the loyalist anti-

Mau Mau Kikuyu chief murdered during the emergency, became one of the parent governors.

At last, women were represented among the non-official governors. Grace Ogot, one of the first African women to become prominent in public life, an eminent author and wife of a Luo professor of history, was one; Josephine Mitchell, foster daughter of the Erskines and onetime secretary first to Derek and then to Gordon Hagberg, and thus conversant with the school's history, was another. Her Canadian husband Frank had come to Kenya to assist in the great African airlifts of the early 1960s so her credentials were impeccable and she had formidable amounts of energy and enthusiasm to contribute.

In an attempt to maintain the school's right to charge higher fees, memoranda were compiled, deputations waited upon the minister and the director of education, and upon the mayor of Nairobi, who happened to be Miss Margaret Kenyatta, the president's daughter. Meetings were arranged, sympathy and understanding of the school's special position were expressed. For a while, optimism rode high, only to be dashed by the implacable attitudes of the city council's education committee.

When little headway appeared to be being made against their demands, Jo Mitchell drew up a memo showing what fees would have to become if the school went independent of officialdom, giving up the council's grant-in-aid. This worked out at 460 shillings per term, or if the original ideal of no more than 25 pupils per class was to be regained, the cost would be 650 shillings per term. While the European and Asian parents – and some of the Africans now risen to well-paid positions – would gladly pay this to ensure continuation of high educational standards, most African parents, often with several members of their large families in school at one time, could not. A comprehensive bursary system would have to be set up if this suggestion were ever adopted.

City council fees, and ours, were set at 250 shillings per term but in mid-1969 they rose to 300 shillings, with an indication that a further rise to 350 shillings was imminent. This prompted a well-reasoned letter of protest from six parents, mostly African but with two unclear signatures which could be Asian names.

And what was this? K.Matiba? But wasn't Ken on our side? Well, he had been, but they were all understandably worried, as was the board, about the effect of rising fees on poorer African parents. Disquietingly, they went further. With 30% African pupils, why were there no African staff? (We knew why. Because only students of lesser achievement opted for this relatively low paid occupation). And should not this proportion become 60%, reflecting the composition of Kenya's population? Other primary schools did not have boards of governors – why this special treatment for Hospital Hill? And please introduce Swahili immediately – which was not at all a bad idea.

This letter was the first shot across the bows of the concept of multiracialism from newly independent and increasingly politicised Kenyans, and it is not insignificant that the four legible signatures to it were all Kikuyus. Until now, the case had been that educating young people of many races and nationalities together would ensure their mutual tolerance and understanding as adults. But what about the effect on those of different tribes? Should it not have been clear that this would be an even greater need in the future in tribally divided Africa?

Some years later when Kenneth Matiba had been placed under detention by President Daniel arap Moi and treated there with horrible cruelty, he emerged a changed man, both physically and mentally, one who, among other things, had become intractably anti-Asian. Recalling the financial help given to the Moi regime by a few Asians, most notably the Hindu involved in the Goldenberg scandal, one can see Matiba had grounds for his antipathy, but it is deeply sad to find this once so able man damning a whole group because of the misdeeds or inadequacies of a few individuals.

American aid had been a lifeline for Hospital Hill School at a crucial stage. Even Ford Foundation, with settler pressure neutralised at independence, reversed its earlier policy and stumped up a welcome $5,000 at one moment of crisis. (The fact that the foundation's then representative in Kenya, David Anderson, had children in the school, meant that they were very aware of its needs.) By 1970, the children of eight American diplomats (and those of many other foreign ones) were on the roll. All this was warmly welcomed at the time. But, if one stopped to think, there was an inevitable corollary.

As early 1962, after Jim Ruchti had replaced Gordon Hagberg as the American representative on the board of governors, John had had to point out that the board could not guarantee a place for every American child. It was clear that, with the stability promised – or at least, hoped for – by independence, more and more Americans and other nationalities, would find business conditions in Kenya attractive, and that their embassies and business enterprises would expand. If all their offspring came to Hospital Hill, this could cause havoc with the racial parity which was at the school's heart. The Americans addressed themselves to this future need, and the International School of Kenya (ISK), built in a most salubrious location amongst acres of coffee beyond the attractive suburb of Spring Valley, became operational by the mid-1960s. Once the school was fully established, America would have no further need for Hospital Hill.

I can recall being mildly incensed at the time by the school's title. It was no more international than any other school in the new Kenya, where, by law now, any nationality must be eligible to enter whatever school they chose. And in its early days, ISK followed exclusively the North American educational system, only in more recent times including the international baccalaureate syllabus in the last two years of its secondary course. This, being more broadly based, ensures that its graduates are prepared for entry into higher education in any country in the world.

Another criticism was that fees were payable in dollars, so few local Kenyans could afford them, fewer and fewer as the Kenyan economy later deteriorated and devaluation of the Kenya shilling increased the cost of an education at ISK. Wealthy African pupils from other countries, such as Uganda, were at that time glad of ISK, and a scholarship system was set up to encourage some Kenyan participation.

But, title apart, one could not argue with the Americans' right to safeguard the welfare of their subjects. Other countries too came to appreciate that if their nationals were to take advantage of business opportunities offered under the new regime, provision for their children's education must have priority. Very soon Nairobi boasted a Japanese school and a French school of high quality. Others followed. The opportunity for a truly multi-racial secondary school was lost for ever.

Relations with the city council

Even had the loss of American input not occurred, Hospital Hill had problems. Though initially co-operative in their dealings with the board, city council officers knew the school was endeavouring to disentangle itself from its relationship with the council's Education Department. They made the council's presence, and indeed its position of authority, more and more plain.

In the old days, all grant-aided primary schools received from the Education Department 80% of the salaries they paid to teachers. After independence this was reduced to 40%. At the end of 1971 it was 'increased from 55% to 60 %'. Then it was reduced once more to 40%. This appeared to be the main reason for the school owing to the city council by mid-1972, the sum of 39,483 shillings and 15 cents! Raising fees by a relatively small amount would soon have redeemed the situation, but the city council would not agree, in spite of measures worked out to subsidise poorer parents. It became clear as time went on that the council had become more and more politicised. In fact, John had resigned as an alderman soon after independence when the newly elected African councillors made it their first task to vote themselves substantial salaries over and above the long-established attendance allowances. The old concept of voluntary service to the community had gone and that of benefiting oneself replaced it.

To be fair, Joel Wanyoike must have been having other difficulties. He and his staff were launched on an entirely new enterprise, taking over from the Ministry of Education the administration of over 70 primary schools in Nairobi municipality, ranging from the old high grade European schools through the middle-ranking grant-aided Asian ones, to the low quality and overcrowded African ones in what had been designated the African locations. His main concern must have been to provide a better education than had been available under colonial rule for the African masses. Against that background he must be considered as having shown great tolerance and understanding of Hospital Hill's position when he first took over.

But the relationship between the school and Wanyoike's city council was anomalous. When David King and later Stanley French were recruited from Geneva, their contracts had been with the board of governors. Two years later French's was transferred to the city council. David had been getting more and more restless and at the board meeting in February 1967 he announced that he would not be renewing his contract and would leave Hospital Hill in April the following year.

He cited as his main reason the 'make do' attitude of the city council, who had long ago promised him a new teacher recruited from overseas – they were having to adopt this policy anyway to compensate for the paucity of well-trained teachers for their own schools after the neglect of the colonial years. Eventually he had managed to find a local teacher to fill the gap, but unless he and the board were able to recruit directly, he foresaw endless difficulties and delays in the future. Furthermore, this laissez faire policy was going to result in lowering standards and he feared that his own children's future would be jeopardised.

Two months later David's contract was transferred to the Ministry of Education, which was not going to let an outstanding graduate teacher leave Kenya if he could be persuaded to stay. (This change had to be sanctioned by the principal immigration officer.) In due course, after leaving Hospital Hill, he became the head of a teacher training college at the coast, but assured John that if ever our problems were sorted out, his dearest wish was to return as headmaster of a school expanding to include a secondary section.

However, in October, he was still at Hospital Hill, complaining again of the difficulty of finding suitable teachers, and Stanley French was congratulated by the board for running the school so efficiently during David's absence on leave. The ministry must have soothed him, and Wanyoike been ameliorative, for the board's minutes reveal that David attended their last meeting, with his replacement Andrew Grigulis in attendance at the end of 1970, departing thereafter to Shanzu Teacher Training College in Mombasa. Grigulis too had been recruited with the help of Desmond Cole-Baker in Geneva and held similar qualifications to David King's.

However, the awful truth soon became apparent. If our teachers were in fact employed by the city council, the city council could do what it liked with them, such as transfer them to other schools under their jurisdiction. When this in fact happened with a Mr Lax, John protested vehemently, and Wanyoike wrote to reassure him that a similar fate would not befall Andrew Grigulis.

In addition to matters of staffing and the setting of fees, bones of contention with the council were its proposal to introduce zoning, whereby children in the city would have to attend a school within easy distance of their home, and its policy on the size of classes. Hospital Hill had always insisted that this should not

177

exceed 25, and while in the old premises off Hospital Hill Road it had not always been possible to accommodate even that many because of the small size of the rooms, pressure was now on to increase class sizes to 35. And indeed, increases had already happened in some of them in David's day. Zoning would cut right across the school's policies, and Wanyoike yielded on this one.

All in all, the city council and Hospital Hill formed an uneasy alliance, and divorce was in the runes from the moment of union. How could the school continue aspiring to provide an education of private school standards while preserving a level of fees which an average African parent could afford? The need for high standard schools would soon be met by private enterprise. Banks proliferated in Kenya after independence, vying with each other to ingratiate themselves with the new elite, and many black Kenyans were encouraged to take out 100% loans for business developments.

The end of the road

Tom Mboya was gone by now, murdered in July 1969 in the centre of Nairobi by a then unknown Kikuyu gunman (he was eventually hanged for the murder), thought by many to have been a paid hitman. Kenya thereby lost its greatest hope for the future, and Hospital Hill a powerful ally. But Charles Njonjo, now attorney general, was still in there fighting for the school. In June 1972 he wrote to the minister of education, J N B Osogo, quoting from a letter of John's emphasising the need for the ministry to remove the school from city council jurisdiction, both in the interests of its development and because of 'the proposed International School idea'. Charles referred to 'the problems we have been having with the Nairobi City Council, and the fact that most councillors have introduced politics into the running of schools'.

By September there was still some hope of a resolution of the problems. Writing to all parents, John explained that the crisis had arisen because of the board's efforts to maintain the high academic and other standards – without increasing fees. 'Active steps,' he wrote, 'are being taken to pursue simultaneously a number of possible alternatives and we are very hopeful that a final decision will be made before the end of October.' He reiterated the board's commitment to maintaining the principles which had always characterised the school, and added how touched the board members were by the dedication and devotion of parents and staff.

In October, 20 teachers wrote to John expressing their continuing concern and a total lack of faith in the city council administration – which had taken nine months to assess salaries, during which time staff had had to exist on basic pay. It did not augur well for the future and they urged that the school should go private.

But the death knell came in November, when the minister wrote pointing out the obstacles, only too evident, which precluded such a move. Most importantly, the government owned the land on which the school stood, and some of its fixed property. Added to this, there was a growing debt, already over £8,000, to the city council, and fee structure must not result in 'the virtual exclusion of Kenyans'. It was the end of the road. When John came home with the news I could not suppress tears. Cheer up, he said, we set out to prove something, and we proved it. Hospital Hill served its times, but times have changed.

The PTA chairman, Chris Obura, and treasurer, J A Hurrell, wrote on the last day of December to say that 'all the outstanding capital debts incurred in the construction of the swimming pool have now been paid'. In accordance with the agreement originally made between the board of governors and the PTA the pool was thereby given to the board on behalf of the school. It had been a wonderful achievement by all concerned and became an enormous asset to future pupils.

The handover of the school completed, in February 1973 John was invited to address the AGM of the PTA. Joel Wanyoike, Nairobi's principal education officer was also asked to speak. He 'pledged to endeavor to maintain the school's racial balance, high ratio of teachers to pupils, and qualified teaching staff'. Several parents, including Ken Matiba, 'rose up to say that the special quality of Hospital Hill School depended largely on its qualified teaching staff, and the parent body wished to see the teachers properly paid and assured of their jobs so that they might continue to maintain the high standards of the school'.

Anne da Gama Rose (formerly Innes) had, in spite of the demands of a young family, courageously agreed to take on the job, *pro tem*, of acting headmistress (Andrew Grigulis had moved on) and had some heartening news: Hospital Hill had again come first in the Common Preliminary Examinations (CPE) and had entered 1973 as a full three-streamed school of 683 pupils and 31 teachers. (The racial breakdown in 1972 had been 34% Asian, 26% European, and 39% African). Echoing the words of J F Kennedy at his inauguration as President, Anne urged that in the coming year the programme should be one of 'not what the school can do for you but what you can do for the school'. The future did not seem entirely bleak.

The view of one member of the audience

Stanley Meisler, an American, was one of the parents present at the PTA meeting that February night. He was also a journalist. A short time later an article under his byline appeared in the *Los Angeles Times*, headlined 'Kenya School Sees Threat to Multiracialism'.

Meisler began: 'The Parent Teacher Association of Hospital Hill School held its annual general meeting the other night on a note – sometimes muted, sometimes not – of racial suspicion. Most parents came to be reassured. Hospital Hill is a unique school in Africa, perhaps in the world. It is multiracial in a calculated way... one third black, one third Asian, one third white.'

He went on to describe the school's history, the white settlers' strict colour bars which existed at the time of its inception, and the current worries that a black council would not keep the strict multiracial policy, wanting only another elementary school for the masses of black children in independent Kenya.

He referred to John's speech – 'I would not do anything to hurt the school,' Karmali said, trying to quiet the suspicions of the parents. Though Karmali was 'a persuasive speaker,' parents would not make up their minds until 'Joel Wanyoike, an African who is chief education officer of Nairobi City Council' had spoken. 'Wanyoike... a dapper and smooth man, Western in manner and dress... obviously wanted to reassure the parents. But to do so he had to overcome a prejudice of the white parents. Whether they admit it or not, most whites in Nairobi believe that blacks, at least at this stage of their development, are less competent than the white expatriates who work here.'

'The feelings of white parents are vital to Hospital Hill,' Meisler continued. 'Without the white parents, there can be no multiracial school. They have as much control over the school's future as the black City Council.' It was a telling point.

Meisler elaborated on the fact that though whites could afford to send their offspring to expensive private schools that catered almost exclusively to foreign white children, it was the chance to have their children mix with those of other races in a good school which attracted them. They could easily drop out.

He spoke of the opening 'a few years ago' of Nairobi International School 'by educators from San Diego... with an American curriculum and high-salaried American teachers'. Despite the pleas of US Ambassador Robinson McIlvaine,

Americans began pulling their children out of Hospital Hill and putting them in the almost all-white American school. The chance for high quality American education seemed more important to most American parents than the chance for a multiracial education. By now, McIlvaine and the Peace Corps director, Bob Poole, were the only American government officials with children still at Hospital Hill. But other foreign white children soon took the places of the transferred Americans.

'Wanyoike,' said Meisler, 'had a difficult time trying to persuade parents to have confidence in the City Council.' Teachers, many of them white expatriates, who were sharing the platform with Wanyoike and PTA officials, produced a litany of bitter complaint. In spite of promises to the contrary, the city council was paying them salaries lower than they had been paid before, and private schools in the city were offering a great deal more. Many of them stayed at Hospital Hill because of their own commitment to multiracialism.

Asserting that problems were due to difficulties in transition, Wanyoike promised that all would be sorted out, but added 'testily' that the 'question of salaries is a matter between teachers and the board, not something for a public meeting'.

'In fact,' Meisler continued, 'the computer mixup and the cavalier attitude of Wanyoike only confirmed the stereotypes that many whites have about African civil servants.' Parents were further troubled when Wanyoike, looking at white and Asian staff, said that he hoped that as soon as possible, the staff 'would more closely reflect the national character of Kenya'. It was the old, old story. 'African students at Teacher Training Colleges of Kenya,' Meisler pointed out, 'are the secondary school pupils who have failed to score high enough in their examinations to go on to advanced secondary school and university. Most come from tribal rural backgrounds and have little knowledge about the world outside Kenya. Since it is not their native language, they speak English poorly.' White parents interpreted Wanyoike's remark 'as a threat' and even some African parents said they worried that Africanisation might lower standards. Their children often spoke a tribal language at home and benefited from sitting in a class where both the teacher and some of their classmates were native speakers of English.

There was considerable ambivalence. One African parent with children at both, warned that primary schools with African staffs were of lower quality than Hospital Hill. 'In a long discourse, he then ridiculed African teachers and even accused them of being drunkards.' This, not surprisingly, dismayed other African parents who 'could hardly sit in a meeting with white and Asian parents and applaud that kind of remark, true or not'. 'Africanisation,' added Meisler, 'is an emotional issue here,' and that 'was a traitorous remark during a night of racial tension.'

Hilary Ng'weno, 'a well-known African writer,' tried to ease the tension and take the emotion out of the issue by suggesting that the city council induce well-educated Africans to teach at Hospital Hill by paying them high salaries. Wanyoike's response was that the council would pay the same salaries to African teachers no matter where they taught. 'You do not have to induce a Kenya teacher to teach a Kenya child in Kenya.'

The arguments continued and Wanyoike was 'badgered with question after question about standards'. Feeling beleaguered and annoyed, he struck back at this critics. 'We have agreed to maintain the standards of the school,' he said 'but what do we mean by standards? We mean the ratio of teachers to pupils, the quality of the teachers, the international character of the school. But by standards, we do not mean European standards. This is a Kenya school. And along that road it will be pushed.'

As the meeting ended, depression reigned. Maybe, the white parents felt, they had been hasty, and blinded by their own racial prejudices. They had failed to convince Wanyoike of the need for a multiracial school. After all, it did little for the Kenyan school system. 'It might be good public relations and it might satisfy the

183

needs of white parents. But if it also meant trouble and a lot of slurs on the qualifications of African teachers, Kenya could do without it. Wanyoike had also been too hasty and prejudiced. He had been attacked again and again by white parents and had probably interpreted this less as a concern for multiracialism than as a demeaning of African abilities and intentions.'

Meisler concluded, 'A multiracial school is a delicate thing. It can work only if all races have confidence in each other. There was little of that the other night at the annual general meeting of the Hospital Hill School PTA.'

So, the experiment was over. We had proved that children educated together from an early age failed to notice the colour of their classmates' skins, learnt to live and play together, were totally tolerant of each other's different cultures and religions, in fact were often interested to learn more of them.

Their parents, meeting at PTA meetings, and when delivering and collecting their young from each other's parties, became friends, and were also involved in the learning and tolerance of other ways and cultures. Not only races, but nations and tribes had learnt sympathetic understanding. Was this not a sound basis on which a new nation might be built?

It was sad that it ended as it did, but the fact was that Kenya was a predominantly African country and parity of races in all schools was unrealistic. We could only hope that Hospital Hill might serve as an example of racial and tribal amity. The school rapidly filled with African pupils, run as any other city council school. Its first African headmaster, Julius Njoroge, was a good man who kept Hospital Hill's results high in the examination league tables. However, with less financial support from wealthier parents, extracurricular activities slowly diminished – apart, thanks to the PTA of the glory days, from swimming.

What some former pupils think

In an ideal world it should be possible to discover and record how Hospital Hill School pupils look back on their time there. Unfortunately, although many remained in Kenya, many others dispersed world-wide, and no old pupils association was ever formed. Those whose whereabouts are known are, almost invariably, very busy people with little time to search their memories and assess the school's significance, if any, on their lives.

However, a few of the earliest students have recorded their impressions and it is clear that they look back upon their years at Hospital Hill as special. At least one of them, Margaret Ross, felt Hospital Hill's quality was due partly to its small size, a valid comment. I quote from pupils of the African, Asian and European communities.

First, Yusuf Keshavjee, a highly successful Indian businessman, who came to Kenya at the age of eight from the shadow of apartheid South Africa, and, though well-travelled, still lives in Nairobi. The school was about to move to its new home in Government House grounds and, with about a dozen pupils, was unlike anything he had previously experienced at the 200 pupil Indian Primary School in Pretoria. In South Africa, he says, he had been too young to experience the bitterness of life under the apartheid regime, but had lived the agonies fully through his parents.

At the time, South Africa was closer culturally to the USA than the UK, and he felt very 'different' when he got to Hospital Hill. Though at first, largely because of his accent – 'I used to say "mulk" instead of milk and "pun" instead of pin' – he was the butt of ridicule, it was always in a friendly manner. 'All my school friends,' he says, 'made me feel so much at home and made it their duty to anglicise me from my American/Afrikaner ways and dressing.' They were so successful that in three years he won a

Kenya-wide elocution contest. Having not been allowed to have any contact with whites –'boers'- in South Africa, finding his teachers and fellow pupils 'unbelievably friendly' was like being on another planet. He recalls 'an all-pervading sadness and feeling of emptiness' during the period after Janet Rainey's death, and has to this day, through his Rotary Club, been active in an anti-polio drive which is part of the world-wide aim to eradicate the disease.

'Ethics, good behaviour, and good habits were of paramount importance to Mrs Walke … She drummed into us all that the truth should always be told irrespective of the consequences.' Yusuf was dismayed to have to return to the segregated school system when his time at primary school ended, separating him from his 'good friends Marsden [Madoka], Jan [Karmali], Udi Gecaga, Judy and Martin Reiss,' but delighted that in recent years there have been opportunities to renew their friendship. He concludes that the fact that many of those pupils have excelled in life 'is in no small measure due to our schooling at the first multiracial school in this country . . . it has influenced my ongoing efforts throughout my life to break artificial barriers that separate and divide people.'

Judy Reiss (now Roper), with her brother Martin and sister Jackie, were the first white pupils at Hospital Hill and both sisters have written vividly and at length about their time there, which Judy describes as 'fun and enjoyable'. 'Through lessons such as history and geography,' she says, 'we were introduced to each other's cultures, religion, dress, food, etc. For example, I can remember the dancing concerts we put on – Jackie and I did a ballet show which we had choreographed ourselves (must have been awful), and had even taught ourselves to go on points.' She recalls African traditional dances, but most of all, the Asian ones, when 'Zelobia and Zulie taught me how to do the dance with the intricate hand movements … I was allowed to put on a sari.'

John Reiss, Judy's father, privately christened Mrs Walke

'Walkie-Talkie', and it is true that she was rarely lost for words. 'She made us feel proud of our school,' says Judy, 'and there was the feeling of one big happy family. We were in a venture together and were very close to each other. I think that was because the lessons included talking about our different cultures and backgrounds so that we got to know a lot about each other.' She also recalls a lot of parent involvement.

After speaking of individual pupils of each race whom she liked and admired, Judy goes on to wonder why she has lost touch with them all, and concluded that one is more likely to continue friendship with friends of one's teenage years. 'A reunion,' she says, 'would be fantastic.'

She did find that her academic level was on the low side when she left Hospital Hill for the Delamere Girls' High School, a totally white establishment in Nairobi. Her peers' reaction to her having come from an inter-racial school was one of disbelief and horror. When she tried to explain how special it was, and what super friends she had made there, 'this only made me an outcast … they saw Africans as their servants who lived in poverty and had to be treated as such, to be kept under control because of the Mau Mau.'

But later in life she was able to tell people about the school, and found only interest. 'It may not have been first class academically,' she adds, 'but in every other respect it was fantastic and what a good grounding for life … [it] had a lasting impression on me and I will always remember it as the best.'

When she was 15, Judy's father was posted to South Africa and the whole family moved there. She eventually became engaged to a South African. Returning later for her wedding, she suddenly realised she could not tolerate his racial views, and three weeks before her wedding, broke off the engagement. The man she has now been married to for 30 years ' has not an ounce of racial prejudice in him'.

Her parents' brave decision to support the first multiracial school in Kenya is one she values, 'as it has enhanced my life'. She ends with the words 'I can't believe the prejudices that still exist in the world.'

Jackie Reiss (now Price) endorses all her sister says, still recalling the names of all her fellow pupils. When other friends heard that the family was going to Hospital Hill, they thought it a bad idea, but says Jackie, 'we listened to Mum and Dad's wise counselling on multiracial schooling and certainly did not live to regret it.' She concludes, 'Of all the 16 schools I have attended during my school days, I've always rated Hospital Hill as my favourite – it certainly put the fun into learning.' The greatest thing was the integration of different cultures, though it is clear that Mrs Walke, with her strong moral code, and her informal teaching methods (spelling bees, nature study disguised as a picnic in the arboretum), was an inspiration to her pupils. Gloria Hagberg also gets a mention in Jackie's account. 'She [in addition to teaching] took the Friday afternoon sing-song sessions and taught us all the words of 'Home on the Range' – which held me in good stead at many a sing-song over the years!'

Jason Likimani was the first Kenya Maasai to qualify as a doctor. He and his dynamic Kikuyu wife, Muthoni, sent their two daughters Sopiato and Soila to Hospital Hill, where they were registered as Sophie and Sheila. (Both, in adulthood, reverted to their distinctive and attractive Maasai names.) Both went on to become professional women, Sopiato a dentist and Soila a pharmacist. Soila, separated from her Ethiopian husband, now lives very happily with her grown-up children north of the Arctic Circle in Canada, a far cry from the Kenya savannah of her father's people

I asked what difference, if any, she felt Hospital Hill had made to her life. Being multiracial, she says, has enabled her always to feel comfortable with people of other races. It was different in that it was a very nurturing environment, like a family, and 'brought out the best in me'. 'If I had not gone there,' she says, 'I should be someone else. I feel I owe my identity to Hospital Hill School.' Bonds formed there have lasted a lifetime.

Interestingly, Soila's time at the school was mainly during the period of Mrs Angus's headship and her most striking memory illustrates Mrs Angus's strength of character. 'One day she was writing on the board and a child pointed out to her that she had made a mistake. She turned her head round and firmly said, "I never make mistakes". Now, how many of us can say that?' asks Soila. 'She also taught me that "nice" is **not** a nice word, and one only uses "get" when referring to getting out of bed. I think of her almost every week of my life consequently, and I quote her often.' These memories cast an interesting sidelight on the contrasting methods of those two early headmistresses.

Soila pays tribute to those who made Hospital Hill School possible and feels it had 'a profound influence on many, an influence which has spread to many parts of the world. ... It represented an ideal world. Children need to know what "normal" is for all our sakes.' 'I have,' she says, 'taken trouble to make sure that my children grow up in a multiracial environment. I have therefore passed on to them the Hospital Hill legacy.'

Margaret Ross (now Margaret Hancock, a teacher), has slightly less rosy recollections, but vividly remembers, in Mrs Walke's day, the extended playtimes. 'I am sure they were not QUITE as long as I remember them – a couple of hours – nor that supervision was QUITE as non-existent, but it certainly led to a wonderful, imaginative, creative education, which I am sure is entirely missing from the lives of the children I now teach, who are watched and supervised every second of the day. I am profoundly grateful for that experience.' She guesses that had she gone to one of the all-white schools, she would have been more steeped in the colonial outlook that all that was worthy started and ended in Britain. As it was she accepted that Hospital Hill school was 'normal'.

She ends by expressing gratitude to her parents for their vision and courage in sending her to Hospital Hill. 'It produced people,' she says, 'who knew that they were worth something , who knew that achievement was available to them if they wanted it, and who had the chance to learn that working together and playing together was possible and positive, before they learnt that society deemed it difficult and negative.'

Amadea Bailey's mother, Marjean, who was so active in the PTA in the early 1960s, recently recalled one of those fund-raising Saturdays celebrating the differing cultures and cuisines of the three races, when she found herself next to an Asian parent, watching the crowds mingle and laugh with each other. In heavily accented English and with eyes bright with tears, she had said to Marjean, 'I never thought I should live to see anything like this in Kenya.'

Amadea's own memories are of 'a feeling of ease, comfort and contentment … and two wonderful friends … I remember not only the easy integration of races and backgrounds but also the easy interaction between boys and girls – we seemed like lion cubs playing amicably together … in such sharp contrast to [my] next school in the US'. But Africa itself – the light, the colours, the feeling of expansion and freedom, the textures – all had a profound and lasting effect on her chosen career as a fine art painter.

The name of Marsden Madoka has already appeared in these pages as one of the first African pupils of Hospital Hill. Now Kenya's Foreign Minister, he nevertheless found time to answer my questions about what, if any difference going to Hospital Hill had made to him, and of any particularly vivid memory he had of those days.

First, he said, he learnt to appreciate that all human beings, irrespective of colour, creed, or race are the same. Competing on equal terms with other children in lessons and games, 'and being able to excel in certain areas better than the European and Asians, whom we had been made to consider superior, gave me a lot of self-confidence in my own ability. I believe,' he added, 'that self-confidence is the most important determinant of a person's future … I have no doubt in my mind that the self-confidence which I developed at Hospital Hill School is responsible for the various achievements I have made in my life.'

Marsden's most striking memory is of the cultural shock of his first day at school, seeing all those children of different colours being able to speak English, 'while I wasn't … However I soon overcame that because at that early age I had no other inhibitions. In fact, mingling at that age was the best way of breaking the racial barriers.'

He concludes that by 'breaking down the racial barriers which existed at that time [Hospital Hill School] therefore has a very special place in the history of Kenya'.

Kassie McIlvaine's father was the American ambassador to Kenya in the early 1970s, at the time when David King was headmaster and Nairobi City Council eventually took over Hospital Hill. Her parents were resolute in not moving their children to the International School of Kenya, as most other American parents had done. Like Margaret Ross, she does have a vague recollection of a non-white classmate being bullied at one time – but cannot remember why. She has observed 'that other people who attended single race schools, especially those predominantly European, feel they have to go out of their way to prove that they have friends, from the early days of their lives, from other races. I do not feel this way … perhaps because I attended Hospital Hill, I feel that friends are friends and race does not matter.'

Kassie still lives mainly in Kenya and feels proud to have gone to Hospital Hill. 'When asked by Kenyan friends where I went to school they are always impressed when I say I went to Hospital Hill, perhaps because it showed an effort by my parents to avoid having us fall into the scene of the surrounding "European" schools.' Are, she wonders ex-Hospital Hill pupils better citizens because of attending such a school? As my son Peter says, it was all a very long time ago.

Tazim Verjee lives in Florida where she is an editorial associate to a world-renowned American scientist. Her father, Kassam Kanji, was one of the founders of the Co-Racial School so she is one of the original pupils, who moved to Hospital Hill in 1953. Although she was less enamoured of Mrs Walke than some (and indeed left for the States some two years later), she speaks with feeling of her pride in her family's involvement in the school, which sprang from her father's belief in the need for a good education which emphasised the study of and respect for the cultures and languages of other races. 'I have benefited tremendously in my career,' she says, 'and learned early in life the true meaning of human diversity.' She cherishes 'the wealth [my] parents gave me' in sending her to such a school.

Due to a recent chance meeting in Canada, Stanley French, who came to teach at Hospital Hill in 1965, has recorded how different the school was from one in east Belfast where he had previously taught. He had moved 'from an all-white society torn apart by the torment and bitterness of religious and political conflict to a school founded on principles of tolerance and respect.' He remains a great admirer of David King, the then headmaster, who worked so hard to implement the vision of the founders – and concludes by wondering how his old students have survived the political turmoil of the past years.

A postscript

When Mrs Walke first arrived in Nairobi in the early 1950s to take up her post as headmistress, she lived for a time at the old Woodlands Hotel. Here she got to know another recent arrival, Marjorie Cooke, who had been recruited by the Crown Agents to work on the accounts of the Posts and Telecommunications Section of the three territories, Kenya, Tanganyika and Uganda, which then comprised the East African High Commission. They formed a friendship which was to last until Eileen Walke's death, and Marjorie provided a sympathetic ear when Eileen relaxed in the evenings, and perhaps let off steam about the problems of her day.

One reason Mrs Walke had been interested in working in Kenya was that her brother, Norman Aitkin, was an officer in the Kenya police, stationed in Nairobi. She one day mentioned to him her concern at the inadequacy of sports training at Hospital Hill. Knowing that the then welfare officer of the police, one Hal Partridge, was a graduate of Loughborough University, specialising in physical education, Norman asked if he would consider some spare-time help to coach the boys in cricket.. Hal, full of energy and enthusiasm (and already critical of the racial segregation he found in Kenya), said he would be delighted. In due course he was invited to tea with Eileen, where he met her friend, Marjorie Cooke. Before very long, they were married.

Hal and Marjorie had ringside seats for the turmoils and triumphs of Hospital Hill School's early years and felt a strong bond with it and especially with the memory of Eileen Walke. To celebrate their 40th wedding anniversary, they returned to the country they had both loved, and naturally enquired about the school's present status.

Marsden Madoka was by then a high-profile figure in Kenya and Hal managed to contact him. Marsden gave a dinner party where they met several ex-pupils, including Yusuf Keshavjee, and learnt something of the present condition of Hospital Hill School, now, of course, no longer in Arboretum Road but situated in Parklands. The buildings and playing fields, not to mention equipment, were manifestly in need of improvement.

With great generosity the Partridges offered financial help in improving the facilities of the cash-strapped city council-run school by erecting an extra classroom and a domestic science block to be called the Eileen Walke Memorial Building. Back home in Malta they awaited further news from Nairobi on progress with the plans but when after several reminders there was no satisfactory response, they withdrew their offer.

Still determined to honour Mrs Walke's memory they returned to Nairobi two years later and went along to Arboretum Road to the original site where she had been headmistress. By now a city council nursery school, intended primarily for the children of workers at State (previously Government) House, the small pupils were of course all Kenyan. The Partridges were appalled by the school's state of neglect. For want of repair, the building seemed on the point of collapse, toilets and washbasins were broken, there was no longer a telephone, water was almost unobtainable and, perhaps worst of all, they were less than impressed with the teaching standards, even though the teachers clearly loved their pupils and longed to do better for them.

The Partridges resolved to provide the finance to remedy all these ills. Thanks to their extraordinary generosity, and with assistance on the spot from Yusuf Keshavjee and Marsden Madoka, not only is the building repaired and modern teaching equipment installed, but special training for staff, provided largely by Hal and Marjorie themselves, has brought it up to first class standards. In July 1998, H E the President of Kenya, Daniel arap Moi, graciously opened the restored and refurbished State House Nursery School. (Did he, I wonder, recall that his own children had been pupils there nearly 40 years earlier?). In a short speech, Hal went further. He magnanimously announced that his two sons, who were present, would continue the family's financial support in the future. Through the President's intervention, the water supply and a new telephone line have been restored.

At the school's gate there now stands a board commemorating the country's first non-racial school and all those who contributed to its success, and in particular in memory of Eileen Walke, headmistress 1953–1957.

Thanks to the Partridges, and retrospectively to Eileen Walke, in those same modest wooden huts a new generation of Kenya children are receiving a better start in life than would otherwise have been the case. Some of the children who worked and played there in the past had skins which were white, some were brown, some black. They all learnt to live and play together in a happy and harmonious atmosphere, demonstrating to any who cared to look that this was possible. It matters not that all today's pupils are black. They are all children, part of Kenya's future.

The proverbial hospitality of Sikhs and Hindus is based on the belief that in every human being there is something of God. All men are brothers, declared the prophet Mohamed. Love each other, Christ proclaimed. Is it too much to hope that during the 20 years of its existence the children who went to Hospital Hill, though they received no formal religious instruction within its classrooms, absorbed these principles by example and personal experience, and that, what Soila Tessema called 'the Hospital Hill legacy' will be passed on to their children's children?

As for me, I have learnt that it is a great thing in life to have a cause.